DUNE AND MOORLAND LIFE

By LEIF LYNEBORG

Edited in the English Edition by
ARNOLD DARLINGTON

Colour plates by
HENNING ANTHON

BLANDFORD PRESS

LONDON

First English language edition 1973
© 1973 Blandford Press Ltd,
167 High Holborn, London WC1V 6PH

ISBN 0 7137 0638 4

Originally published in Denmark as
HVAD FINDER JEG I KLIT OG HEDE
by Politikens Forlag 1972
World copyright © 1972 Politikens Forlag A/S
8 Vestergade, Copenhagen

Translated from the Danish by
Kirsten Campbell-Ferguson

Colour printed in Denmark by
F. E. Bording A/S, Copenhagen.
Text printed in Great Britain by
Richard Clay (The Chaucer Press) Ltd.,
Bungay, Suffolk.

PREFACE TO THE ENGLISH EDITION

Like the previous books allied to this one in the Colour Series, *Dune and Moorland Life* this is a Danish publication translated and adapted for an English readership.

The literal translation of the Danish title is retained for that of the English version, although there are comparatively few references in the original to sandy heathlands as we know them. For a book applicable to the British Isles this is something of an omission, and an attempt is made in the descriptive section to fill the gap.

Sandy conditions—at least over extensive tracts—prevail in all three ecosystems, dune, heath and moor. Fundamental differences between duneland on the one part and heathland and moorland on the other result from their origins. Dunes are formed by additive processes, when the velocity of wind-borne particles of sand and other maritime solids is reduced by obstacles, notably the shoots of plants, so that sandhills build up. Heathland and moorland result from subtractive processes, when highly energized climaxes like forests are destroyed and fail to regenerate. Dunes commonly metamorphose to become increasingly productive and, because of the calcium carbonate derived from shell fragments, to become more or less basic. Heaths and moors both accumulate peat which inhibits aeration of the underlying soil and gives it a sour (acidic) reaction. A hard layer (pan) develops below the surface and this resists penetration by the roots of large plants and tends also to inhibit drainage. Distinction between heath and moor is that of degree rather than of nature: the layer of peat is shallow on a heath and deep on a moor and one form merges into the other. The author uses a common term for both. Of the two, what we call heathland is the more likely to be represented at the lower levels of ground in Britain.

Although a minority of the species included here have not been reported as British, nearly all are so closely related to forms which are known to occur that they are useful for purposes of general identification. It cannot be too strongly emphasized that there is a need constantly to maintain a watch for those which, although hitherto unrecorded, might well turn up from time to time. In some cases, Danish ecological information is the best available on a particular species, and in these cases material relevant to Denmark has deliberately been retained in the English edition. This will add to the usefulness of the book to those with more advanced interests and, with the growing tendency for schoolchildren as well as adults to travel abroad, may increase its relevance for many others.

A list of works suggested for further reading is given at the end of the book.

Arnold Darlington,
Malvern College.
February 1973

INTRODUCTION

This book, describes the fauna of dunes and moorlands, i.e. parts of the countryside which are lacking in true tree growth and are characterized by being warm and arid. Like previous books in this series, the present describes only the invertebrate fauna, from worms and centipedes to insects, spiders and slugs. It is comparatively easy to define the fauna of dunes and moorlands in relation on the one hand to the fauna of the foreshore and on the other to the fauna of dry fields and commons. Consequently only a few species have been included from earlier books.

The 48 colour plates fall into two parts. The first 45 show a section of the varied fauna of dunes and moorlands. It must be emphasized that this is merely a cross-section: nevertheless the book covers a greater proportion of the total number of species than in the case of *Woodland Life* and *Field and Meadow Life*. Animals are arranged according to the zoological system, beginning with worms, centipedes and millipedes, continuing with various insect orders, and ending with spiders, snails and slugs. Various development stages of a number of species, and their nests, webs, etc., are also shown. The last three plates give examples of the galls caused by insects and mites on certain typical moorland and dune plants. The drawings in this section are arranged according to the botanical system. In the text under the plates the scientific name of the animal causing the phenomenon has been given in brackets. Data on the galls is provided in the notes.

Supplementary information in the descriptive sections includes references to size, since the various animals could not always be drawn to a common scale. Information also includes the status of an animal in Britain and elsewhere, and something about its feeding and breeding habits.

Information has been derived from a number of Danish an other reference books, and in addition valuable contribution to the book have been made by several Danish zoologists. It a pleasure to acknowledge the cooperation of the following Kåre Fog; Karen Hammer, M.Sc.; Knud Th. Holst, M.A. Ove Jensen; N. P. Kristensen, M.Sc.; Søren Langemark, O Lomholt, E. Torp Pedersen, M.A., and Niels L. Wolff, B.Eng

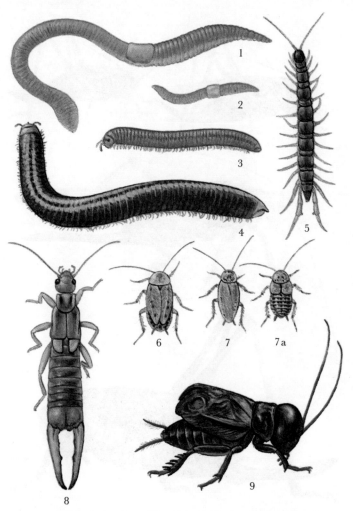

EARTHWORMS, MILLIPEDES, CENTIPEDES, COCKROACHES,
EARWIGS AND TRUE CRICKETS

1 Marsh Worm, *Lumbricus rubellus* **2 Moss Worm,** *Dendrobaena octaedra*
3 Snake Millipede, *Cylindroiulus friseus* **4 Snake Millipede,** *Archiulus sabulosus* **5 Lithobiomorph Centipede,** *Lithobius calcaratus* **6 Common Wood Cockroach,** *Ectobius lapponicus* **7 Sand Cockroach,** *Ectobius panzeri,* male **7a** female **8 Sand Earwig,** *Labidura riparia* **9 Field Cricket,** *Gryllus campestris*

6

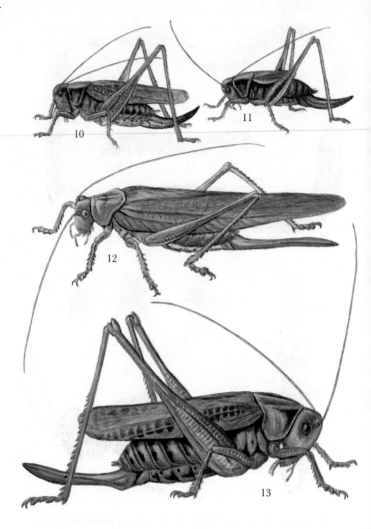

6

BUSH CRICKETS
10 Sand Grasshopper, *Platycleis denticulata* 11 Moor Grasshopper,
Metrioptera brachyptera 12 Great Green Grasshopper, *Tettigonia viridissima* 13 Wartbiter, *Decticus verrucivorus*

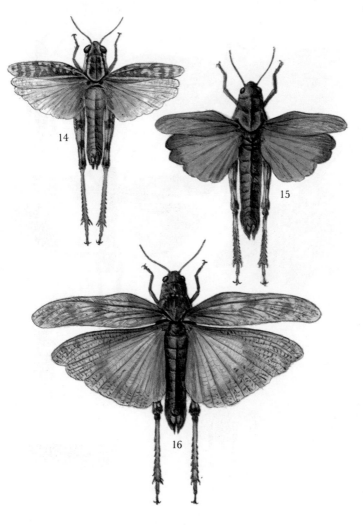

FIELD GRASSHOPPERS
14 Italian Grasshopper, *Calliptamus italicus* **15** *Psophus stridulus* **16** *Bryodema tuberculata*

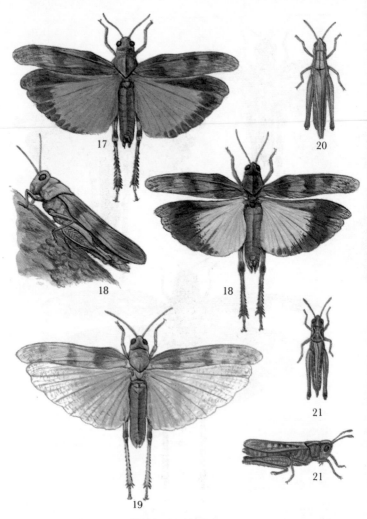

8

FIELD GRASSHOPPERS
17 **Red-winged Desert Grasshopper,** *Oedipoda germanica* 18 **Blue-winged Desert Grasshopper,** *Oedipoda caerulescens* 19 **Blue-winged Steppe Grasshopper,** *Sphingonotus caerulans* 20 **Field Grasshopper,** *Chorthippus albomarginatus* 21 *Myrmeleotettix maculatus*

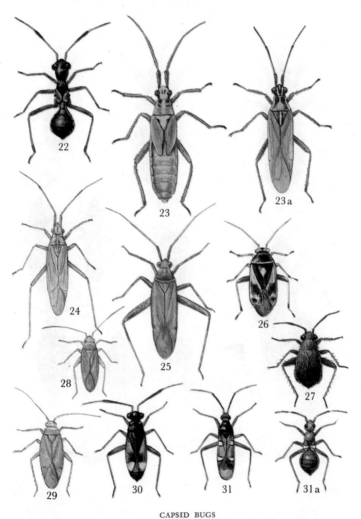

CAPSID BUGS

22 *Myrmecoris gracilis*   23 *Leptopterna ferrugata*, female   23a male   24 *Tri-
gonotylus psammaecolor*   25 *Phytocoris varipes*   26 *Polymerus brevicornis*   27
Orthocephalus saltator   28 *Orthotylus ericetorum*   29 *Orthotylus virescens*   30
Globiceps cruciatus   31 *Systellonotus triguttatus*, male   31a female

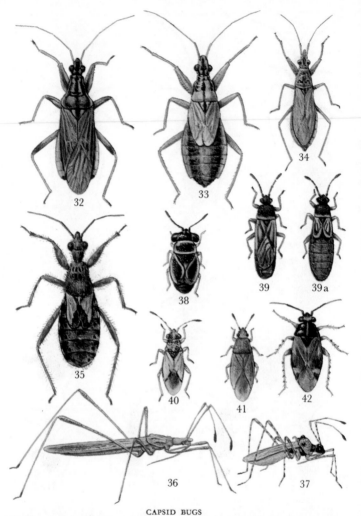

CAPSID BUGS

32 **Great Damsel Bug,** *Nabis major* 33 **Broad Damsel Bug,** *Nabis flavomarginatus* 34 **Heath Damsel Bug,** *Nabis ericetorum* 35 **Heath Assassin Bug,** *Coranus subapterus* 36 *Neides tipularius* 37 *Gampsocoris punctipes* 38 *Geocoris grylloides* 39 **European Chinchbug,** *Ischnodemus sabuleti* 39a short-winged form 40 *Nysius thymi* 41 *Cymus glandicolos* 42 *Monosynamma bohemani*

11

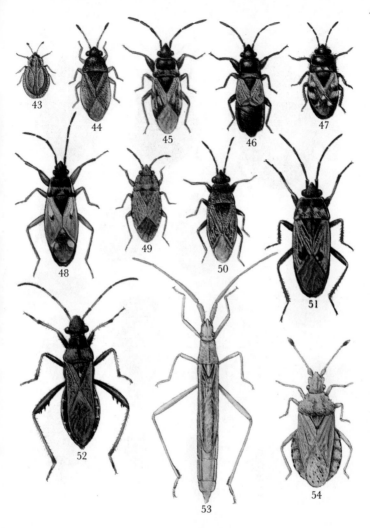

CAPSID BUGS
43 *Acalypta parvula* 44 *Stygnocoris pedestris* 45 *Scolopostethus decoratus* 46
Macrodema micropterum 47 *Pionosomus varius* 48 *Eremocoris abietis* 49 *Goni-anotus marginepunctatus* 50 *Peritrechus geniculatus* 51 *Rhyparochromus pini*
52 *Alydus calcaratus* 53 *Chorosoma schillingi* 54 *Arenocoris falleni*

12

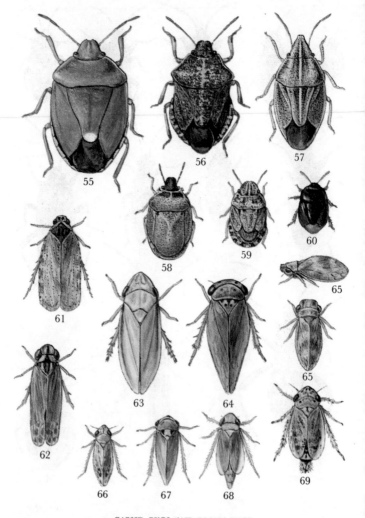

CAPSID BUGS AND PLANT BUGS

55 Juniper Shieldbug, *Pitedia juniperina* **56** *Rhacognathus punctatus* **57
Bishop's Mitre,** *Aelia acuminata* **58** *Podops inuncta* **59** *Sciocoris cursitans*
60 *Legnotus picipes* **61** *Cixius similis* **62** *Ommatidiotus dissimilis* **63** *Neophilaenus pallidus* **64** *Idiocerus lituratus* **65** *Ulopa reticulata* **66** *Psammotettix
exilis* **67** *Macropsis impura* **68** *Mocuellus collinus* **69** *Euscelis plebeius*

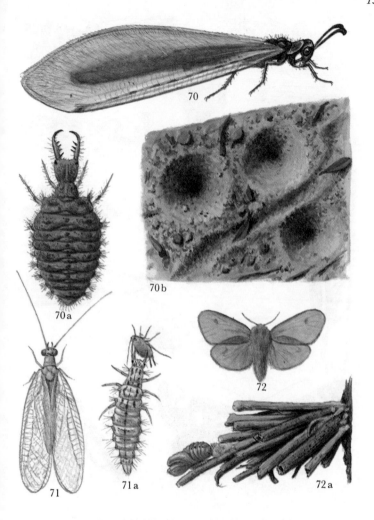

LACEWINGS AND MICROLEPIDOPTERA
70 **Ant-lion,** *Myrmeleon formicarius* 70a larva 70b snare 71 **Green Lace-wing,** *Chrysopa abbreviata* 71a larva sucking aphid 72 **Large Bagworm,** *Pachytelia villosella,* male 72a larval sac

14

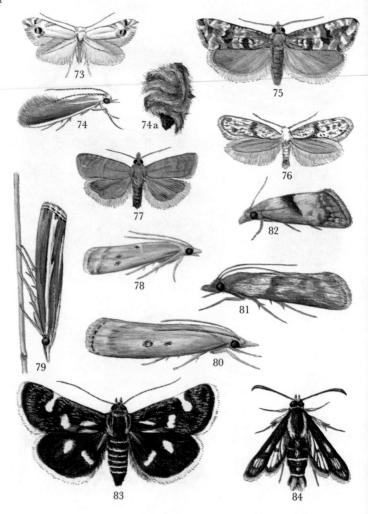

MICROLEPIDOPTERA AND CLEARWING MOTHS

73 **Broom Moth,** *Leucoptera spartifoliella* 74 **Sac Moth,** *Coleophora bilineatella* 74a larval sac 75 *Lobesia littoralis* 76 *Swamerdamia conspersella* 77 *Argyroploce arbutella* 78 *Gymnancycla canella* 79 **Grass Moth,** *Catoptria fulgidella* 80 *Melissoblaptes zelleri* 81 *Selagia spadicella* 82 *Hysterosia hilarana* 83 *Titanio pollinalis* 84 **Thrift Clearwing,** *Aegeria* (=*Sesia*) *muscaeformis*

GEOMETRID MOTHS

85 **European Emerald,** *Thalera fimbrialis* 86 *Rhodostrophia vibicaria* 86a colour variant 87 *Lythria purpurata* 88 *Ortholitha plumbaria* 89 **Narrow-winged Pug,** *Eupithecia nanata* 90 **Grass wave,** *Perconia strigillaria* 91 **Netted Mountain Moth,** *Isturgia carbonaria* 92 **Bordered Grey,** *Selidosema ericetaria* 93 **Common Heath,** *Ematurga atomaria,* female 93a male 94 **Annulet,** *Gnophos obscurata* 95 **Streak,** *Chesias legatella*

16

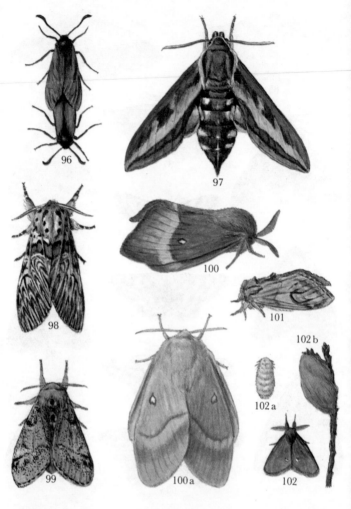

ZYGAENID MOTHS, HAWK MOTHS, AND MOTHS WITH SPINNING LARVAE
96 Transparent Burnet, *Zygaena purpuralis,* mating **97 Bedstraw Hawk,**
Celerio (=*Deilephila*) *galii* **98 Puss Moth,** *Dicranura vinula* **99 Dark
Tussock,** *Dasychira fascelina* **100 Oak Eggar,** *Lasiocampa quercus,* male
100a female **101 Pebble Prominent,** *Notodonta ziczac* **102 Heath
Vapourer,** *Orgyia ericae,* male **102a** female **102b** cocoon

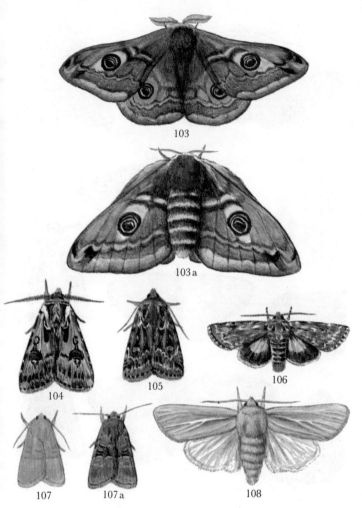

MOTHS WITH SPINNING LARVAE AND NOCTUID MOTHS
103 Emperor Moth, *Saturnia pavonia*, male   103a female   **104 Archer's
Dart**, *Agrotis vestigialis*   **105 True Lover's Knot**, *Lycophotia porphyrea*
106 Beautiful Yellow Underwing, *Anarta myrtilli*   **107** *Oligia literosa*,
Danish west coast variety *onychina*   107a type   **108** *Hyphilare littoralis*

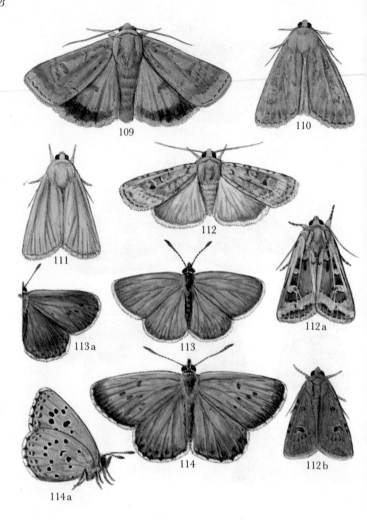

NOCTUID MOTHS AND BUTTERFLIES

109 **Lesser Yellow Underwing,** *Triphaena comes* 110 *Apamea* (=*Hadena*) *sordida engelharti* 111 **Lyme Grass,** *Arenostola elymi* 112 **Coast Dart,** *Euxoa cursoria* 112a and 112b colour variants 113 *Maculinea alcon,* male 113a female 114 **Large Blue,** *Maculinea arion* 114a underside

BUTTERFLIES

115 *Fabriciana* (=*Argynnis*) *niobe*   115a underside   116 **Queen of Spain Fritillary,** *Argynnis* (=*Issoria*) *lathonia*   116a underside   117 **Grayling,** *Satyrus* (=*Hipparchia*) *semele*, female   117a male   118 **Wall butterfly,** *Pararge* (=*Lasiommata*) *megera*

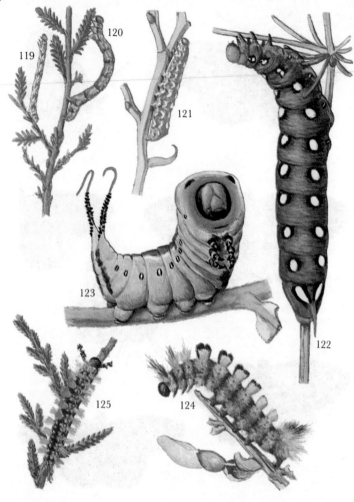

MOTH LARVAE

119 **Narrow-winged Pug,** *Eupithecia nanata* 120 **Common Heath,**
Ematurga atomaria 121 **Beautiful Yellow Underwing,** *Anarta myrtilli*
122 **Bedstraw Hawk,** *Celerio* (=*Deilephila*) *galii* 123 **Puss Moth,**
Dicranura vinula 124 **Dark Tussock,** *Dasychira fascelina* 125 **Heath
Vapourer,** *Orgyia ericae*

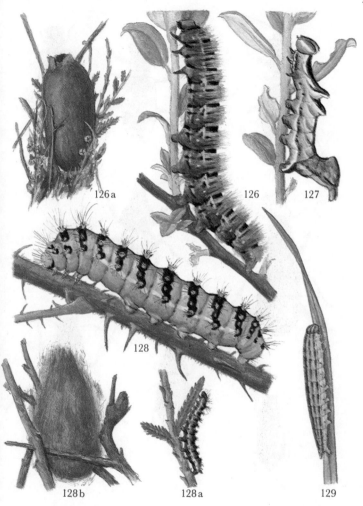

MOTH AND BUTTERFLY LARVAE
126 **Oak Eggar,** *Lasiocampa quercus* 126a cocoon 127 **Pebble Prominent,**
Notodonta ziczac 128 **Emperor Moth,** *Saturnia pavonia,* fully-developed
larva 128a larva in 1st instar 128b cocoon 129 **Grayling,** *Satyrus*
semele

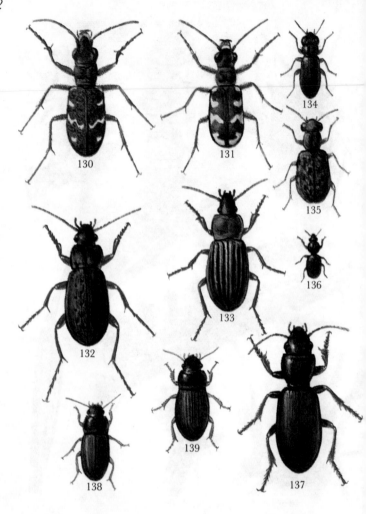

CARNIVOROUS BEETLES AND GROUND BEETLES
130 **Wood Tiger Beetle,** *Cicindela sylvatica* 131 **Brown Tiger Beetle,**
Cicindela hybrida 132 *Carabus arvensis* 133 *Carabus nitens* 134 *Notiophilus
aquaticus* 135 *Elaphrus riparius* 136 *Dyschirius obscurus* 137 *Broscus cephalotes*
138 *Harpalus smaragdinus* 139 *Harpalus rubripes*

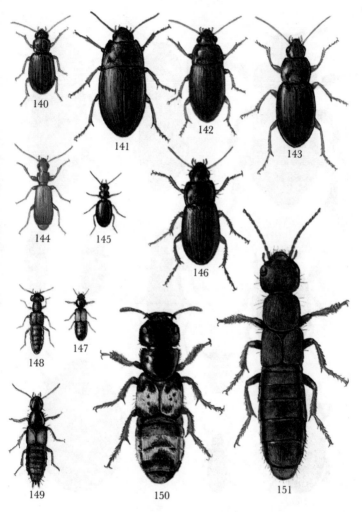

GROUND BEETLES AND ROVE BEETLES

140 *Bradycellus harpalinus* 141 *Amara spreta* 142 *Amara bifrons* 143 *Calathus mollis* 144 *Dromius linearis* 145 *Metabletus truncatellus* 146 *Pterostichus punctulatus* 147 *Bledius arenarius* 148 *Stenus geniculatus* 149 *Philonthus varians* 150 *Creophilus maxillosus* 151 **Devil's Coach-Horse,** *Ocypus (=Staphylinus) olens*

24

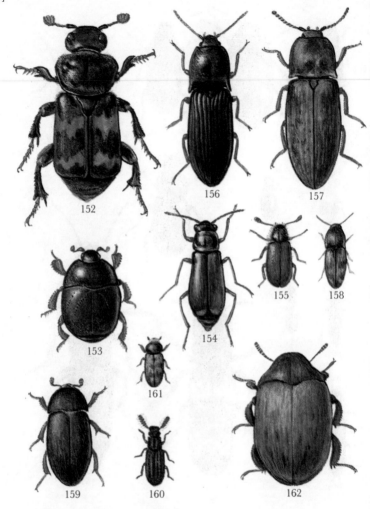

BURYING BEETLES, ROVE BEETLES, SOFTWINGS AND CLICK BEETLES
152 Sexton Beetle, *Necrophorus interruptus* 153 *Saprinus semistriatus* 154
Malachius viridis 155 *Necrobia violacea* 156 *Corymbites aeneus* 157 *Lacon
murinus* 158 *Cryptohypnus pulchellus* 159 *Dermestes laniarius* 160 *Orthocerus
clavicornis* 161 *Heterocerus fusculus* 162 *Byrrhus pilula*

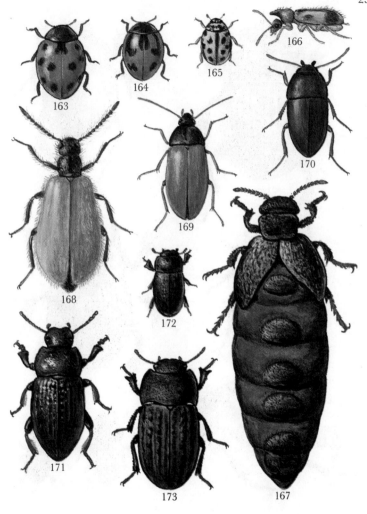

25

LADYBIRDS, OIL BEETLES, AND NOCTURNAL GROUND BEETLES
163 **Eleven-spot Ladybird,** *Coccinella undecimpunctata* 164 *Coccinella hieroglyphica* 165 **Sixteen-spot Ladybird,** *Tytthaspis sedecimpunctata* 166 *Notoxus monocerus* 167 **Oil Beetle,** *Meloë variegatus* 168 *Lagria hirta* 169 *Isomira murina* 170 *Crypticus quisquilius* 171 *Phylan gibbus* 172 *Melanimon tibialis* 173 *Opatrum sabulosum*

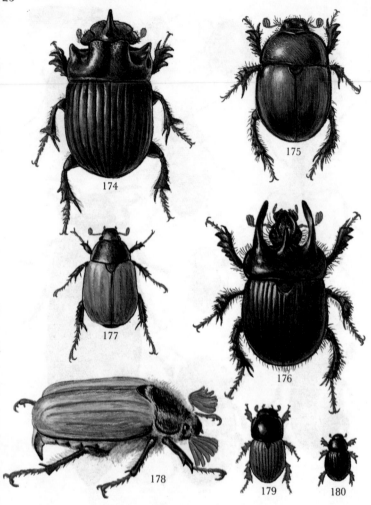

DUNG-BEETLES AND CHAFERS
174 *Copris lunaris* 175 **Bumble-dor,** *Geotrupes vernalis* 176 **Minotaur Beetle,** *Typhaeus typhoeus* 177 **Dune Cockchafer,** *Anomala (Euchlora) dubia* 178 **Cockchafer,** *Melolontha hippocastani* 179 *Aphodius foetens* 180 *Aegialia arenaria*

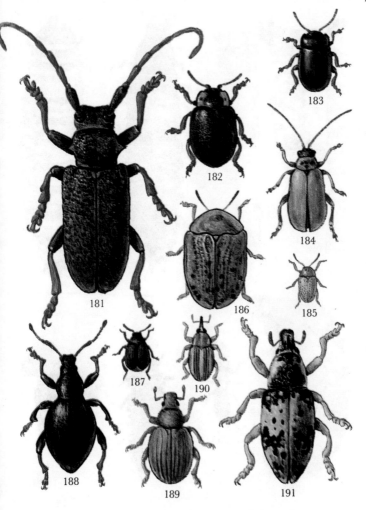

LONG-HORNED BEETLES, LEAF BEETLES, PEA 'WEEVILS' AND
TRUE WEEVILS
181 **Willow Longhorn,** *Lamia textor* 182 *Melasoma collaris* 183 *Chrysomela
analis* 184 *Lochmaea suturalis* 185 *Cryptocephalus fulvus* 186 *Cassida
nebulosa* 187 *Bruchidius fasciatus* 188 *Otiorrhynchus atroapterus* 189 *Cneorrhinus plagiatus* 190 *Tychius venustus* 191 *Cleonus fasciatus*

28

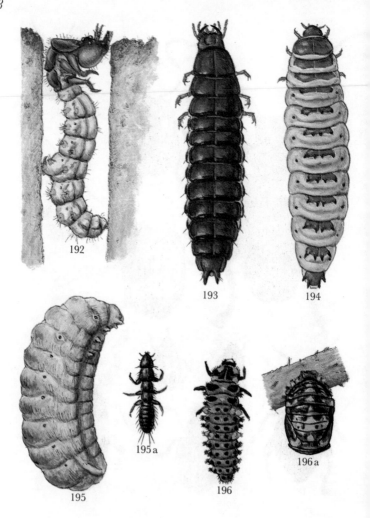

BEETLE LARVAE – CARNIVORES
192 **Brown Tiger Beetle,** *Cicindela hybrida* 193 **Ground Beetle,** *Carabus arvensis* 194 **Sexton Beetle,** *Necrophorus interruptus* 195 **Oil Beetle,** *Meloë variegatus,* pre-pupa 195a young larva 196 **Eleven-spot Ladybird,** *Coccinella undecimpunctata* 196a pupa

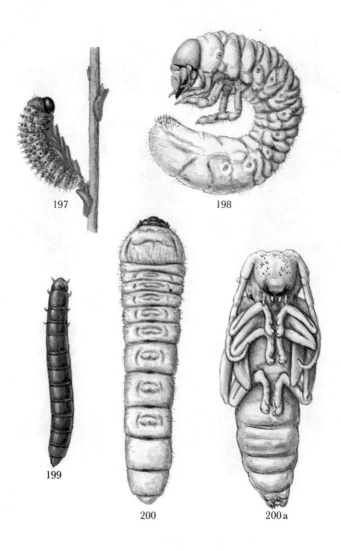

197   198

199   200   200a

BEETLE LARVAE – HERBIVORES

197 Leaf Beetle, *Lochmaea suturalis*   **198 Dune Cockchafer,** *Anomala dubia*   **199 Nocturnal Ground Beetle,** *Opatrum sabulosum*   **200 Willow Longhorn,** *Lamia textor*   200a pupa

ICHNEUMONS, SOLITARY AND SOCIAL WASPS, AND TRUE ANTS
201 *Banchus compressus* 202 **Ruby-tail,** *Hedychrum nobile* 203 **Red Wasp,**
Vespa (=*Paravespula*) *rufa* 204 **Potter Wasp,** *Eumenes pedunculatus* 205
Pterocheilus phaleratus 206 **Spiny Mason Wasp,** *Odynerus spinipes* 207
Formica rufibarbis, worker 207a queen 208 **Negro Ant,** *Formica fusca*
209 **Black Ant,** *Lasius niger.*

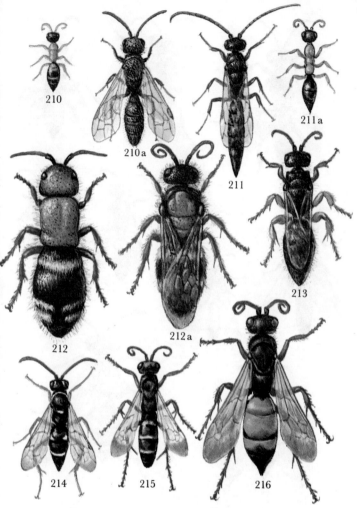

31

VELVET 'ANTS' AND SPIDER-HUNTING WASPS
210 **Black-headed Velvet-ant,** *Myrmosa melanocephala,* male   210a female
211 **Ant-wasp,** *Methoca ichneumonides,* male   211a female   212 **Large
Velvet-ant,** *Mutilla europaea,* female   212a male   213 *Tiphia femorata*   214
Spotted Ceropales, *Ceropales maculata*   215 **Leaden Spider Wasp,**
Pompilus plumbeus   216 **Dark Anoplius,** *Anoplius fuscus*

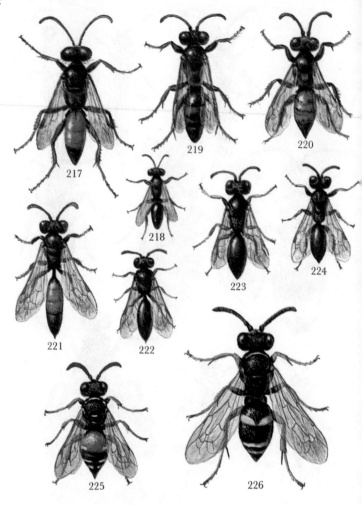

DIGGER WASPS

217 *Astata stigma* 218 *Miscophus ater* 219 *Tachysphex ibericus borealis* 220 *Tachysphex pompiliformis* 221 **Two-coloured Mimic Wasp,** *Psen equestris* 222 **Pale-footed Black Wasp,** *Psenulus pallipes* 223 **Melancholy Black Wasp,** *Diodontus tristis* 224 *Passaloecus roettgeni* 225 *Nysson maculatus* 226 **Large Spurred Digger,** *Nysson spinosus*

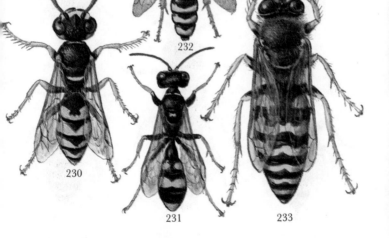

DIGGER WASPS
227 **Common Sand Wasp,** *Ammophila sabulosa* 228 **Great Sand Wasp,**
Podalonia viatica 229 **Two-girdled Digger,** *Argogorytes mystaceus* 230
Bee-killer Wasp, *Philanthus triangulum* 231 **Field Digger Wasp,** *Mellinus
arvensis* 232 **Sand Tailed-digger,** *Cerceris arenaria* 233 *Bembix rostrata*

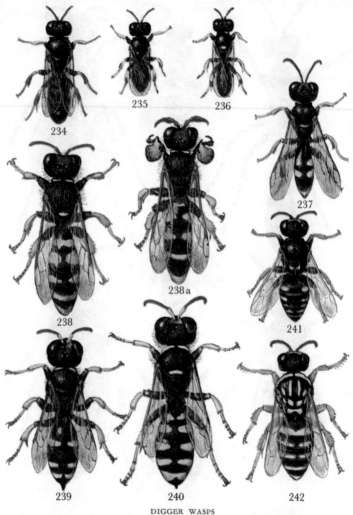

DIGGER WASPS

234 *Lindenius albilabris*   235 *Entomognathus brevis*   236 **Wesmael's Digger**,
Crossocerus wesmaeli   237 **Four-spotted Digger**, *Crossocerus quadrimaculatus*
238 **Slender-bodied Digger**, *Crabro cribrarius*, female   238a male   239
Ectemnius continuus   240 **Big-headed Digger**, *Ectemnius cavifrons*   241
Common Spiny-digger, *Oxybelus uniglumis*   242 *Oxybelus lineatus*

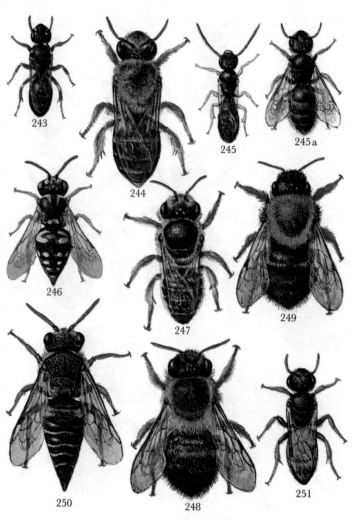

35

SOLITARY BEES

243 *Hylaeus confusa* 244 **Girdled Colletes,** *Colletes succinctus* 245 *Halictus tumulorum*, female 245a male 246 *Epeolus variegatus* 247 **Silvery Leaf-cutter,** *Megachile argentata* 248 **Leaf-cutter,** *Megachile circumcincta* 249 **Mason Bee,** *Osmia maritima* 250 *Coelioxys elongatus* 251 *Sphecodes pellucidus*

36

SOLITARY AND SOCIAL BEES
252 **Nomad Bee,** *Nomada flavopicta* 253 **Nomad Bee,** *Nomada rufipes*
254 *Panurgus banksianus* 255 **Hairy-legged Mining Bee,** *Dasypoda hirtipes*
256 **Mining Bee,** *Andrena fuscipes* 257 **Mining Bee,** *Ahdrena hattorfiana*
258 **Mining Bee,** *Andrena vaga* 259 **Bumble-bee,** *Bombus variabilis* 260
Heath Bumble-bee, *Bombus jonellus*

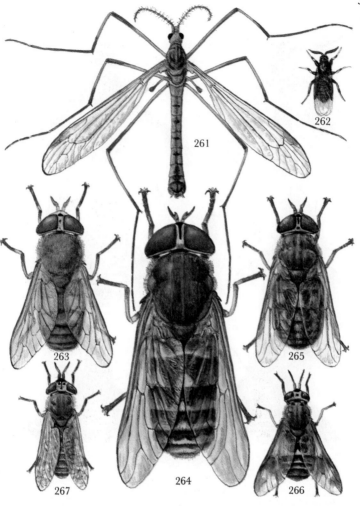

37

CRANE-FLIES AND CLEGS

261 **Daddy-long-legs,** *Tipula juncea* 262 *Aspistes berolinensis* 263 *Atylotus rusticus* 264 *Tabanus sudeticus* 265 *Hybomitra montana* 266 **Thunder-fly,** *Chrysops relictus* 267 **Gad-fly,** *Haematopota pluvialis*

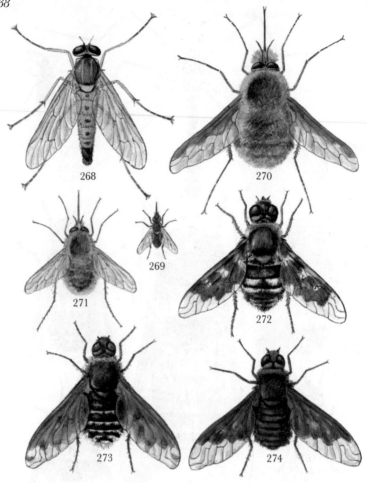

SNIPE-FLIES AND BEE FLIES
268 *Rhagio tringaria* 269 *Phthiria pulicaria* 270 **Great Bee Fly,** *Bombylius major* 271 *Systoechus sulphureus* 272 *Thyridanthrax fenestratus* 273 *Anthrax anthrax* 274 *Hemipenthes morio*

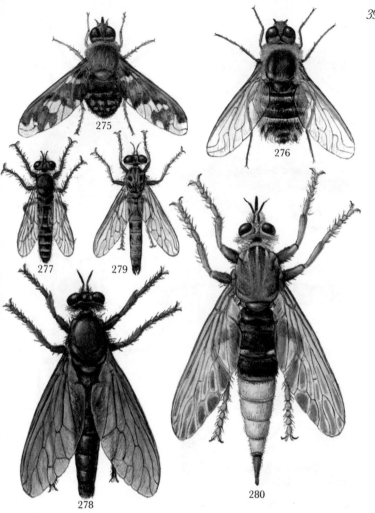

39

BEE FLIES AND ROBBER FLIES
275 *Exoprosopa capucina* 276 *Villa modesta* 277 *Lasiopogon cinctus* 278
Dasypogon diadema 279 *Rhadiurgus variabilis* 280 *Asilus crabroniformis*

40

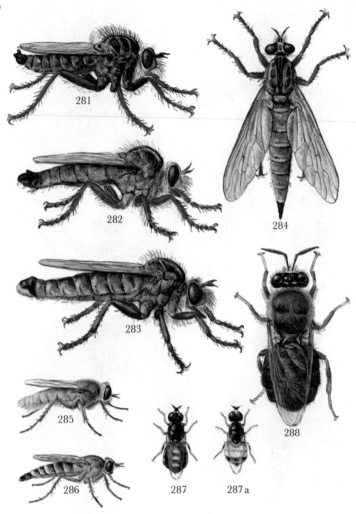

ROBBER FLIES, STILETTO FLIES AND SOLDIER FLIES
281 *Dysmachus trigonus* 282 *Machimus rusticus* 283 *Antipalus varipes* 284 *Philonicus albiceps* 285 *Thereva annulata* 286 *Thereva marginula* 287 *Nemotelus uliginosus*, female 287a male 288 *Stratiomys longicornis*

41

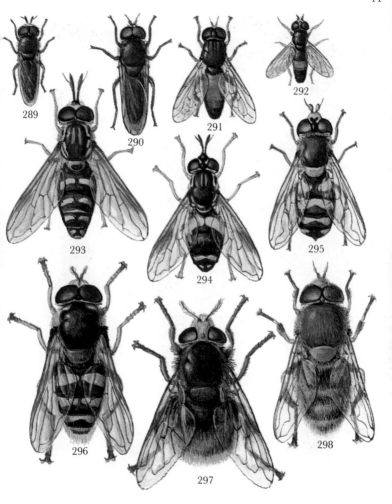

HOVER FLIES
289 *Pipizella varipes* 290 *Chilosia mutabilis* 291 *Eumerus sabulonum* 292
Paragus tibialis 293 *Chrysotoxum festivum* 294 *Chrysotoxum bicinctum* 295
Didea intermedia 296 *Sericomyia silentis* 297 *Volucella bombylans* 298
Drone-fly, *Eristalis intricaria*

42

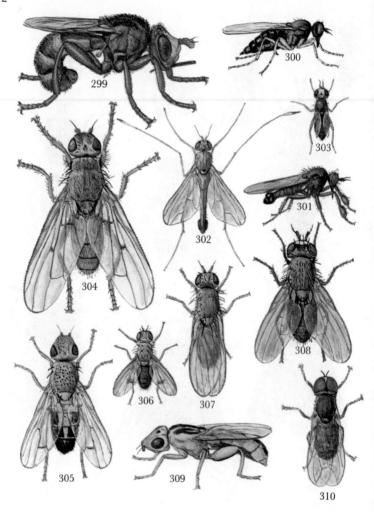

THICK-HEADED FLIES, EMPIDS, LONG-HEADED FLIES, SHORE FLIES,
FRIT FLIES, BIG-HEADED FLIES, ETC.
299 **Wasp-fly,** *Sicus ferrugineus* 300 *Platypalpus strigifrons* 301 *Hilara
lundbecki* 302 *Sciopus loewi* 303 *Striphosoma sabulosum* 304 *Helcomyza
ustulata* (=*Actora aestuum*) 305 *Tetanops myopina* 306 *Trixoscelis obscurella*
307 *Chamaemyia* (=*Ochthiphila*) *flavipalpis* 308 *Minetta desmometopa* 309
Frit-fly, *Meromyza pratorum* 310 *Alloneura littoralis*

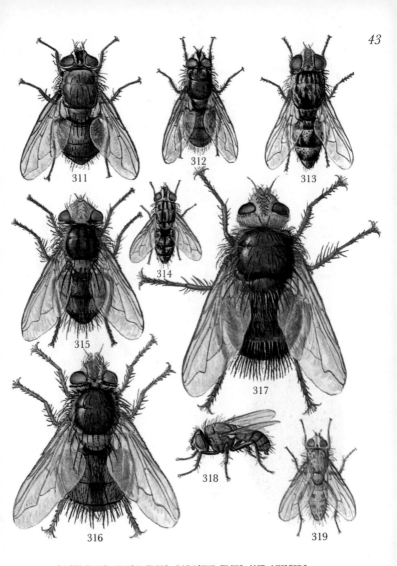

BLOW-FLIES, FLESH FLIES, PARASITE FLIES AND MUSCIDS

311 **Green-bottle,** *Lucilia sericata*   312 *Melinda agilis*   313 *Miltogramma punctatum*   314 *Metopia leucocephala*   315 *Salmacia (=Gonia) ornata*   316 *Larvaevora (=Echinomyia) fera*   317 *Larvaevora (=Echinomyia) grossa*   318 *Phorbia penicillaris*   319 *Helina protuberans*

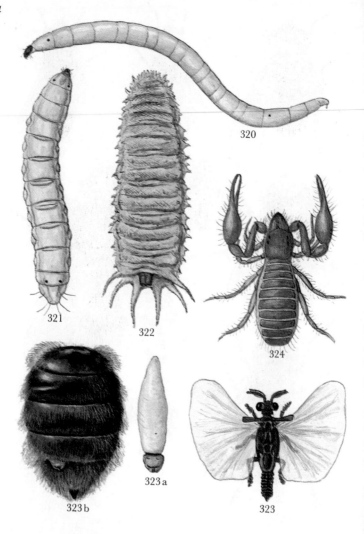

FLY LARVAE, STREPSIPTERA AND FALSE SCORPIONS
320 **Stilleto Fly,** *Thereva* sp. 321 **Assassin Fly,** *Machimus* sp. 322 **Hover Fly,** *Volucella* sp. 323 *Stylops muelleri*, male 323a female 323b female lying in abdomen of mining-bee 324 *Neobisium muscorum*

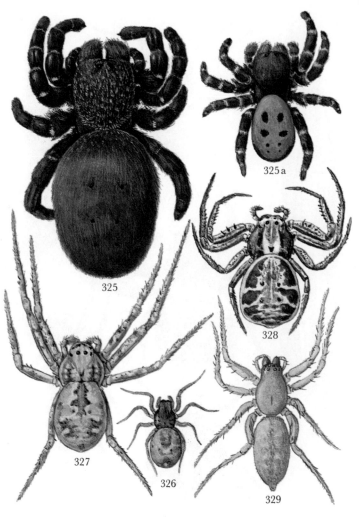

45

SPIDERS
325 *Eresus niger*, female 325a male 326 *Dictyna arundinacea* 327 *Philo-dromus fallax* 328 *Xysticus cristatus* 329 *Clubiona similis*

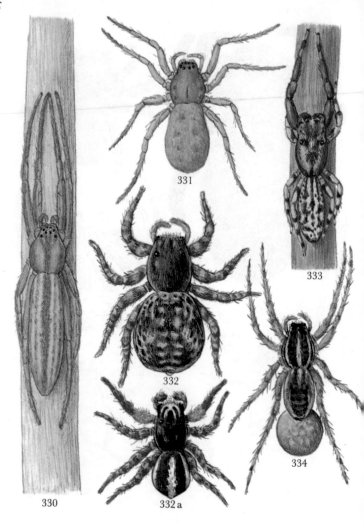

SPIDERS

330 *Tibellus maritimus* 331 *Agroeca proxima* 332 *Aelurillus v-insignitus*, female 332a male 333 *Hyctia nivoyi* 334 *Lycosa monticola*

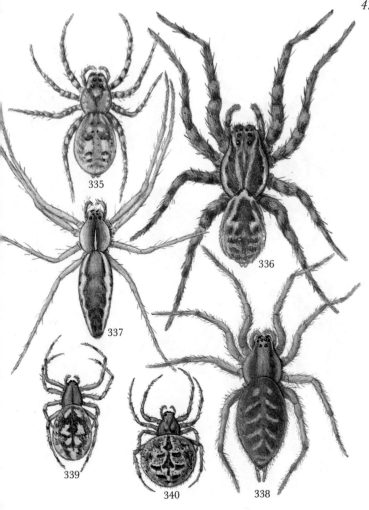

47

SPIDERS

335 *Arctosa perita* 336 *Tarentula fabrilis* 337 *Pisaura mirabilis* 338 **Labyrinth Spider,** *Agelena labyrinthica* 339 *Araneus adiantus* 340 *Araneus redii*

48

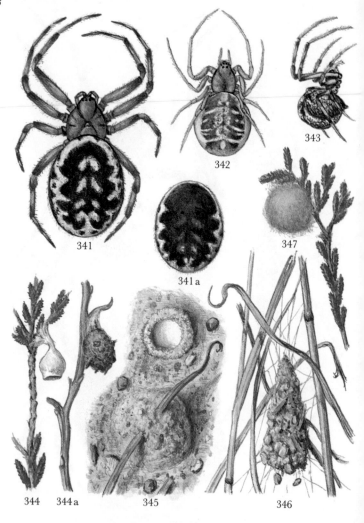

SPIDERS AND SPIDERS' WEBS
341 *Lithyphantes albomaculatus* 341a colour variation 342 *Theridion sisyphium* 343 *Theridion saxatile* 344 *Agroeca brunnea*, egg cocoon 344a egg cocoon covered by soil particles 345 *Philodromus fallax*, egg cocoon before the depositing of the eggs 346 *Theridion saxatile*, retreat 347 *Araneus redii*, egg cocoon

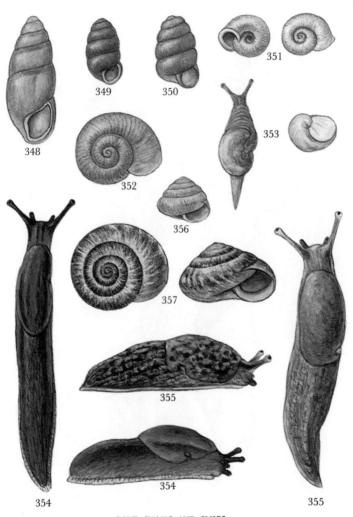

LAND SNAILS AND SLUGS

348 Slippery Moss-snail, *Cochlicopa lubricella*   **349 Chrysalis-snail,** *Pupilla muscorum*   350 *Columella aspera*   351 *Vallonia excentrica*   352 *Nesovitrea hammonis*   **353 Pellucid Glass-snail,** *Vitrina pellucida*   **354 Dusky Slug,** *Arion subfuscus*   355 *Deroceras agreste* and *D. reticulatum*   **356 Tawny Glass-snail,** *Euconulus fulvus*   **357 Wrinkled Snail,** *Helicella caperata*

50

GALLED JUNIPER, SEA COUCH AND CREEPING WILLOW
358 Shoot-gall on Juniper (*Oligotrophus juniperinus*) 359 Cigar Gall on Sea
Couch (*Isthmosoma hyalipenne*) 360 Stem-gall on Creeping Willow (*Euura
atra*) 361 Leaf-gall on Creeping Willow (*Pontania viminalis*) 362 Leaf-gall
on Creeping Willow (*Pontania pedunculi*) 363 Rosette-gall on Creeping
Willow (*Rhabdophaga rosaria*) 364 Shoot-gall on Creeping Willow (*Rhabdophaga jaapi*) 365 Leaf-galls on Creeping Willow (*Eriophyes tetanothrix*)

GALLED BURNET ROSE, BROOM, NEEDLE FURZE, CROWBERRY,
BEARBERRY AND THYME

366 Leaf-gall on Burnet Rose (*Diplolepis* (=*Rhodites*) *spinosissimae*) 367
Auxilliary bud galls on Broom (*Asphondylia sarothamni*) 368 Flower-bud
Gall on Broom (*Jaapiella sarothamni*) 369 Shoot-gall on Needle Furze
(*Jaapiella genisticola*) 370 Shoot-gall on Crowberry (*Aceria* (=*Eriophyes*)
empetri) 371 Bud-galls on Bearberry (*Aceria* (=*Eriphyes*) *jaapi*) 372 Galled
Flowers on Thyme (*Aceria* (=*Eriophyes*) *thomasi*)

GALLED LADY'S BEDSTRAW, WORMWOOD AND HAWKWEED
373 Shoot-gall on Lady's Bedstraw (*Dasyneura galiicola*)   374 Stem-gall on
Lady's Bedstraw (*Geocrypta galii*)   375 Shoot-gall on Lady's Bedstraw
(*Aceria* (=*Eriophyes*) *galiobia*)   376 Stem-gall on Wormwood (*Eucosma* sp.)
377 Capitulum-gall on Wormwood (*Boucheella artemisiae*)   378 Stem-gall on
Hawkweed (*Aulacidea hieracii*)

THE INVERTEBRATE FAUNA OF DUNES AND MOORLANDS

One of the earlier books in this series, *Seashore Life*, describes the animals which are found on the beach as far as the high-water mark and another, *Field and Meadow Life*, describes the fauna of cultivated fields, permanent pastures, meadows and marshes. The present book attempts to cover the areas between these extremes, i.e. the various types of littoral dunes, sandhills, moorland fields and moors: some attention has also been paid to the fauna of slightly damper habitats, like hollows between the dunes and heather bogs.

A moor gives the superficial impression of being a homogenous environment, but there are, in fact, big variations. A main feature of moor vegetation is the various dwarf scrubs. The most common scrub is heather, but crowberry, bell heather, bearberry, bog myrtle and others are also found, and in this book a number of animals are described which are associated with these plants. A thick growth of lichens is often found under the scrub, and this growth gives good protection for various terricolous animals. There are also a number of herbaceous plants which are characteristic of the moor. These, among others, are mat-grass, moss-rush, deer-grass, purple moor-grass, sheep's fescue and wavy hair-grass, all of which have a typical tufted growth. Such tufts of grasses and sedges contain the habitats of a number of small animals, a fact which anyone can verify by digging up a tuft and shaking out its contents. The following plants with colourful flowers can be found among others on the moor: cat's ear, mountain tobacco, goldenrod, devil's bit and tormentil. There is, furthermore, a scattered growth of broom, juniper and needle furze. Such variety does not reflect homogeneity.

Hollows in the ground cause variations in the water content of the soil, and these again cause variations in the vegetation and animal life. Elevated parts of the moorland plains, or heather-covered hills in an undulating countryside, on the other hand, will have a tendency to be more or less free of vegetation. These open areas, varying in size from a few square metres to several square kilometres like the true inland dunes, are of great importance to the fauna, as they give ideal conditions for all digging animals, like bees and wasps, as well as for certain beetles, flies and spiders. These open areas are usually not completely devoid of vegetation, and are often characterized by a small grass, grey hair-grass. Consequently such localities are often called hair-grass hills or hair-grass plains according to their topographical character. The true inland dunes, however, often have completely barren areas, which are windswept plains with yellow sand dunes. This book describes a range of species found in these places; most of these species will be the same animals as those found in the dunes near the coast. The animals which build in the open, loose soil are often dependent on the surrounding vegetation; they can find their food in the flowers or catch their prey in the vegetation.

In seashore dunes, and in the so-called yellow dunes, the sand can be seen everywhere among the vegetation, which mainly consists of grasses like marram grass, lyme grass and couch grass, although other flowering plants are also found. The yellow dune is gradually overgrown with vegetation and becomes the so-called green dune. Marram grass is still common here, but other grasses and sedges, like red fescue and sand sedge, are gaining in importance. All of these have widely spread root systems, which contain the habitats of many insects and their larvae. In the more fertile parts of the green dune, plants like fescue grass and other grasses, lady's bedstraw, biting stonecrop, cat's ear, pansy, thyme, bird's-foot trefoil and chickweed, can all be found, but in the barren parts sand sedge is dominant.

The next step in the development of the dune vegetation is the grey dune. It constitutes an anti-climax to the rich vegetation of the green dune, and the reason is that a gradual leaching of the sand takes place, making it less nutritious for the plants. The vegetation of the grey dune is characterized by a great number of lichen species, which provide the grey coloration, together with sand sedge and grey hair-grass. Often patches of crowberry and heather can also be found. The vegetation of grey dunes is fairly poor in species and approaches the vegetation of the most barren parts of the moor. Topographically, grey dunes often merge into moors lying farther inland.

Various shrubs are commonly found in the dune, mainly sea buckthorn, but also burnet rose: the former is most plentiful in calcareous sand. Creeping willow and juniper are also colonizers.

The main characteristic of the physical environment of dunes is that on sunny summer days the temperature variation between day and night can be considerable, at times up to 50°C. The activity of many heat-loving animals is due to these high temperatures. Some of the species avoid the extremes of the temperature variation by digging themselves in, and it can be generally said that well-developed digging ability is characteristic of many dune forms. The wind is also an important factor. Dune animals include kinds which have adapted themselves to resist wind effects by losing their wings altogether, by having reduced wings, or by having a special ability to cling to the vegetation or to objects on the ground. In short, the environment of the dunes (and this applies also to the drier parts of the moors) can be described as being arid and desert-like, i.e. lacking in easily accessible water, due to the ease with which water passes through the sand, the poor ability of sand to absorb water, and the drying effects of wind and sun.

DESCRIPTIONS AND NOTES

OLIGOCHAETA: Earthworms

1 Marsh Worm, *Lumbricus rubellus*

Length, 10–12 cm. Although this earthworm is found mainly in rich humus soil in woods, it can also be seen in great numbers in the soil of grey dunes, especially in hollows. Sometimes many worms can be found dead at the bottom of a dune hollow. Like other earthworms it lives on dead plant material. It is said to drag leaves into its burrows during the night.

2 Moss Worm,
Dendrobaena octaedra

Length, 3–4 cm. One of the hardiest of earthworms. Lives under moss tufts between the lichen and the upper layer of humus. Very resistant to drought and low temperatures. It is one of the few species found on moors.

DIPLOPODA: Millipedes

3 Snake Millipede,
Cylindroiulus friseus

Length, 15–20 mm. A common millipede found both in dunes and on moors. Like most millipedes it cannot withstand drought, and consequently lurks under stones and similar places during the day.

Millipedes generally feed on rotting plant material. At times, however, some eat fresh roots and other living plant material, and several, among them *C. friseus*, can become pests in greenhouses and nurseries. The group of millipedes to which this and the following species belong lay their eggs in a nest built from small soil particles and the mother's excrement.

4 Snake Millipede, *Archiulus sabulosus*

Length, up to 50 mm. The largest millipede in north Europe. Common in many different places. It endures drought better than other millipedes, and consequently is also to be found in very dry places, such as yellow dunes. It is often seen sitting in the vegetation, but what it is doing there is not known for certain. The number of millipedes of this species varies considerably from year to year, and in some years a migration on a fairly large scale takes place.

CHILOPODA: Centipedes

5 Lithobiomorph Centipede,
Lithobius calcaratus

Length, 10–15 mm. Found in Britain, not Ireland, and said to prefer drier habitats than many centipedes. Common in dry sandy places and found mainly under stones. The centipede is a predatory animal which attacks small soil animals killing these with a pair of poison fangs situated on the back of the head. Eggs are deposited singly and the female covers them with a glutinous secretion to which soil particles may adhere. The male is illustrated in the plate; the female lacks the characteristic protuberances on the hindmost (fifteenth) pair of legs.

ORTHOPTERA: Cockroaches

6 Common Wood Cockroach, *Ectobius lapponicus*

Length, 6–13 mm. Found chiefly in woods, but also frequently to be seen on heaths and moors. Mainly noticed on the ground, but the male, which is a reasonably good flier, also occurs in bushes and trees. Vespertine in activity. The female carries her egg pod around for two days before depositing it on the ground. The nymphs overwinter, and the fully developed insects can be observed from early summer. Probably widely distributed.

7 Sand Cockroach, *Ectobius panzeri*

Length, 5–7 mm. The smallest of the three cockroach species living in the wild in Britain. It is restricted mainly to the maritime counties of East Anglia and the English Channel. Found on both yellow and grey dunes. The female (7a) has short, broad elytra which reach as far as the middle of the abdomen.

DERMAPTERA: Earwigs

8 Sand Earwig, *Labidura riparia*

Length, 13–26 mm. Unmistakable. Almost twice as long as the common earwig, *Forficula auricularia* (see *Field and Meadow Life*, No. 24). Found in sandy places like gravel pits and dunes and under dry seaweed on the shore. In Britain, restricted to one locality near Bournemouth. It digs burrows up to 2 m long in the sand, down to a depth of 30–40 cm. The daylight hours are spent in the burrows. At night this earwig goes in search of prey. It feeds on insect larvae, spiders and other small animals, and differs from the common earwig in this respect, since the latter is mainly herbivorous. Its breeding habits are similar to those of the common earwig.

ORTHOPTERA: True Crickets

9 Field Cricket, *Gryllus campestris*

Length, 17–26 mm. A southern and central European species. It has a scattered distribution in Britain, where it is declining in numbers. It lives on dunes and in dry sandy fields. It excavates burrows in which it lives. The male sits in the opening of the burrow and 'sings' during May and June as a means of attracting the female. After mating the female inserts hundreds of eggs in the soil near the burrow. Over-wintering is as nearly full-grown nymphs.

ORTHOPTERA: Bush Crickets

10 Sand Grasshopper,
Platycleis denticulata
Length, 16–23 mm. This species colonizes dry and warm places. It is found among the sparse vegetation of the dunes and along roads in dune plantations, where it sits in the sun on stones or on bare, sandy patches. It flies fairly well in warm weather and lives on small insects and plant material. In Denmark, common in north Zealand (Tisvilde), Anholt and Bornholm.

11 Moor Grasshopper,
Metrioptera brachyptera
Length, 12–16 mm. In Britain, a species of swamps and bogs as well as of dry places, it frequently occurs in the transition zone between marsh and moor vegetation. The nymphs hatch in May, and the adult insects can be seen until October.

12 Great Green Grasshopper,
Tettigonia viridissima
Length, 22–53 mm. *La cigale* of French children. Widely distri-

buted in Britain and found all over Denmark except in central and west Jutland. The species is well concealed by its uniform green colour, but its presence is betrayed by the 'song' of the male. Stridulation takes place in tall herbs, bushes or trees from late summer to well into October, and can be heard hundreds of metres away. Its rhythm is reproduced by the jingle, 'Katie did, she did! Katie did, she did!' It begins in the late afternoon and continues until a few hours before dawn. Predatory. The female deposits the eggs deep down in the soil. The nymphs hatch in spring and are sexually mature in 3 months. Adults occur from the middle of July.

13 Wartbiter, *Decticus verrucivorus*
Length, 24–44 mm. The biggest of the bush crickets. Very rare in Britain, it is found both in damp and dry situations, but always where there is low vegetation. The 'song', which consists of short, rasping chirps, can only be heard during the day in hot, sunny weather. Omnivorous.

ORTHOPTERA: Field Grasshoppers

14 Italian Grasshopper,
Calliptamus italicus
Length, 15–34 mm. Not British. A south and central European species which is found in warm and dry areas. In particularly hot

summers it can occur in great numbers in limited areas and can cause considerable damage to crops, equal to that caused by the migratory locust. Although, like other field grasshoppers, it moves its hind legs up and down as if stridulating, no sound is caused by this movement. Instead, the species produces its sound by rubbing the mandibles against each other.

15 *Psophus stridulus*
Length, 23–40 mm. Not British. It occurs here and there in Sweden, Norway and Finland as well as in central Europe, but only in such warm places as moors, sandy heaths, hillsides exposed to the sun and dry mountain meadows. During its flight the male produces a loud, rattling sound with its wings which can be heard far away.

16 *Bryodema tuberculata*
Length, 27–36 mm. Not British. Found in small numbers in Denmark, north Germany and Finland on stretches of moorland with low and sparse vegetation. In the Alps it is found in slightly different terrain, e.g. along streams and rivers with little or very sparse vegetation. It flies readily; the flight takes place at a height of 1–5 m and is accompanied by a rattling or humming sound produced by the wings. Prior to mating both sexes appear to stridulate with their hind legs,

but no sound emanates from this movement. It is apparently the actual movement to which the partner responds. Egg cases are placed in the soil. The nymphs hatch the following spring, and the animals are fully developed in late July and early August.

17 Red-winged Desert Grasshopper, *Oedipoda germanica*
Length, 17–28 mm. Found in central and southern Europe and as far as western Asia, where it colonizes hot, arid places like dry, stony hillsides and moors. It is even more restricted to dry habitats than the following species. Only a slight buzz is heard during flight.

18 Blue-winged Desert Grasshopper, *Oedipoda caerulescens*
Length, 15–28 mm. Not British. The species is found in central Europe, and north as far as north Germany and south Sweden. Like the previous species it prefers dry habitats, but it is more tolerant. It is found on dry slopes, in quarries, in dunes, and on heaths, i.e. in places with sparse vegetation. The stridulating movements, which the species makes with its hind thighs, usually do not produce sound, but as an introduction to mating the male sometimes does use them to make sounds. Like the previous species it lives on fresh plant material.

19 Blue-winged Steppe Grasshopper, *Sphingonotus caerulans*

Length, 14–26 mm. Not British. A native of south Sweden and central and southern Europe. Like the two previous species it is a heat-loving grasshopper, which is found in dry, sandy places with sparse vegetation both inland and near the coast. It is the best flier of the central European field grasshoppers. Only a slight buzzing noise is heard during flight.

20 Field Grasshopper,
Chorthippus albomarginatus

Length, 13–18 mm. Widespread in suitable places throughout northern, western and central Europe, but in Britain rather localized. A typical representative of the genus *Chorthippus*, which includes a number of the most common field grasshoppers. Frequently found in damp places, such as hollows in dunes. Another, somewhat similar, dune species is *Ch. brunneus*.

21 *Myrmeleotettix maculatus*

Length, 12–16 mm. A species with clubbed antennae, conspicuously so in the male. In Britain, widely distributed from Land's End to the north of Scotland. Closely associated with sand, and a common insect of dunes, moors and the clearings in plantations. Fully developed at the beginning of July.

HEMIPTERA-HETEROPTERA: Capsid Bugs

22 *Myrmecoris gracilis*

Length, 4–6 mm. Found in Surrey, Hants and Dorset. It occurs sporadically in dry grass-covered places and is one of the many terrestrial bugs which mimics ants. If examined from the side, its proboscis shows immediately that it is a bug. The almost wingless, ant-like shape illustrated here is the commonest form by far, but a long-winged type is also found, which is of importance in the dispersal of the species. The long-winged form has sometimes been found in material washed up on the beach. The eggs over-winter and the fully-developed imagines are seen in July–August. The species feeds mainly on aphids and other small insects. It is also found in anthills, where it is supposed to live on the brood.

23 *Leptopterna ferrugata*

Length, 6·5–8·5 mm. This and the following species belong to the grass bug group of the capsids. The species is common in dry grass-fields, where it sucks the juices of various grasses. There is a distinct difference between the male and the female. The male (23a) has well-developed wings, whereas the female nearly always is very short-winged. The eggs over-winter and the fully-developed animals are found in their greatest numbers in late summer.

24 *Trigonotylus psammaecolor*
Length, 5–7 mm. Found on coastal dunes on lyme grass, often in large numbers. Alive, the animals are blue-green like the leaves of the lyme grass, but after dying they often become yellow-green in colour. Their life cycle is similar to that of the two previous species.

25 *Phytocoris varipes*
Length, 6–7·5 mm. Common in the turf covering dunes and in similar herbaceous vegetation. The female is shorter and not as slim as the male illustrated. It feeds on small animals and on the flowers and unripe fruits of many different herbs. Its life cycle is like that of 22 and 23, but individual adults can be found well into the autumn. The genus *Phytocoris* comprises several species, most of which are associated with various trees.

26 *Polymerus brevicornis*
Length, 4–5 mm. Found in summer among lady's bedstraw on sandhills or very dry soil.

27 *Orthocephalus saltator*
Length, 4–5·5 mm. Distributed throughout the British Isles and associated with various Compositae in uncultivated land and on the coast. Adults occur in summer until August, and the eggs over-winter.

28 *Orthotylus ericetorum*
Length, 3–4 mm. Common throughout the British Isles on heather and bell-heather. When living, easily recognized by the two orange spots on the elytra, but like many other capsid bugs it quickly loses much of its coloration after death.

29 *Orthotylus virescens*
Length, 4–5 mm. Common on broom, often in great numbers. It damages the young leaves, causing numerous small white patches to form. Most abundant in August.

30 *Globiceps cruciatus*
Length, 4–6 mm. Widely distributed in Britain, but local, in dry, sandy places, where it lives on creeping willow, often in association with 42. Its eggs are deposited in cracks in the willow bark and over-winter. Despite the fact that the species is associated with one particular plant, it is mainly predatory. Individuals with fully-developed wings can be found, but the short-winged bug is commoner.

31 *Systellonotus triguttatus*
Length, 3–5 mm. Distributed in Britain south of a line from Lincoln to Carmarthen. There is a big difference between the male and the female. The male (31) has fully developed wings and can look something like a small pompilid when it is running fast. The female (31a), which is nearly always wingless, is an ant-mimic like 22. The species is often found in close association with such ants as

Formica fusca (208) and *Lasius niger* (209). It lives partly on small animals (e.g. aphids) and partly on the sap of various plants, including creeping willow, sheep's fescue, tormentil and heather. Like the previous species, it deposits eggs in crevices.

32 Great Damsel Bug,
Nabis major

Length, 7–9 mm. On the Continent, often found singly in dense marram grass, where it lives close to the ground. The eggs over-winter and hatch in May, and the adult animals can be found till late summer. Species of *Nabis* are predatory and are distinguished by their curved proboscis and strong front legs, which are used for holding the prey, consisting mostly of other insects.

33 Broad Damsel Bug, *Nabis flavormarginatus*

Length, 7–9 mm. Very common and widely distributed in Britain in dry fields. In contrast to the previous species lives higher in the vegetation. As with many other bugs (e.g. 22 and 30) this species is wing-polymorphic, developing both long-winged and short-winged forms. The long-winged type is fairly common in Britain.

34 Heath Damsel Bug, *Nabis ericetorum*

Length, 6–7 mm. Smaller and more reddish-brown than other species of *Nabis* found in this country. Common on heaths and moors throughout Britain. Fully-developed individuals over-winter; but in early summer only the nymphs are found, which look like the adult bugs but are smaller and lack wings. Adults are seen again from mid-August.

35 Heath Assassin Bug, *Coranus subapterus*

Length, 9–12 mm. This, the commonest British assassin bug, occurs on moors, heaths and grey dunes. It resembles a big, hairy species of *Nabis* with a strong proboscis, but actually it belongs to the Reduviids, which also include the big flybug, *Reduvius personatus*, found in houses. The species stridulates. Full-winged individuals are seldom seen. The eggs over-winter.

36 *Neides tipularius*

Length, 10–12 mm. Found in most southern counties and in East Anglia. A slight, straw-coloured bug which is very difficult to see when it remains still, which it does if alarmed. Fairly common in dry situations both on coastal dunes and inland. The adult animals over-winter among dead leaves, etc., and can be found in spring and in autumn. In summer only the nymphs are seen: these have the same shape as the adult insects but are green in colour.

37 *Gampsocoris punctipes*

Length, 4–5 mm. A fragile-looking bug with a scattered distribution in Britain. Like the previous species it is well camouflaged, as its thin legs and antennae are broken up by dark spots. It lives on restharrow, and the adult bug over-winters. The nymphs, seen in summer, are green with heavily spotted antennae and legs.

38 *Geocoris grylloides*

Length, 3·5–4·5 mm. This unmistakable bug is fairly common but is often overlooked when it runs around on the ground among plants in dry places. It over-winters as an adult.

39 **European Chinchbug,**
Ischnodemus sabuleti

Length, 4–6 mm. A bug which has greatly increased in Britain in the last 80 years. Often found in great numbers in dunes. Its principal food plants are lyme and marram grass, where the red nymphs can be found in great numbers in the leaf sheaths. They also over-winter in the sheaths, the adults and nymphs together. On the whole both adults and nymphs can be seen throughout the year, but the adults are the more active. They often crawl on people sunbathing in dunes. The long-winged form is of importance in dispersal.

40 *Nysius thymi*

Length, 3–5 mm. Distributed throughout England and Wales on cindery ground and common on moors and dunes, where it colonizes various plants including heather and thyme. The species lays its eggs in autumn, and the nymphs over-winter.

41 *Cymus glandicolor*

Length, 4–5 mm. Common in most English counties. It lives on various forms of *Carex* (sedge), both in dry places where sand sedge grows, and in dune and heather bogs where there are other species. The adults over-winter. The reddish-brown nymphs somewhat resemble fruits of sedges.

42 *Monosynamma bohemani*

Length, 3–4 mm. Often found in great numbers on creeping willow, and in rarer cases on grey willow. The coloration of this capsid varies considerably; individuals which are almost black can be found. The eggs over-winter and fully-developed individuals occur in July-August.

43 *Acalypta parvula*

Length, 1–2 mm. The smallest and commonest assassin bug in Britain. Assassin bugs can easily be recognized by the fact that their wings are divided into small cells (areas), so as to present a net-like appearance. This species can be found under moss and litter in sandy places. Over-winters as an adult.

44 *Stygnocoris pedestris*
Length, 2–3 mm. One of the commonest of British bugs. A groundbug like the seven species which follow. Mainly found in open situations on light, dry soils with good plant cover. Thought to live on the seeds of various plants. The eggs over-winter. The adults are about from August to late autumn.

45 *Scolopostethus decoratus*
Length, approx. 4 mm. A bright little insect common in heather vegetation throughout most of Britain. Like most groundbugs the adult over-winters. Not much is known about its feeding habits, but it probably eats plant seeds as well as being predatory. It has been seen to suck the body-juices of the capsid *Orthotylus ericetorum* (28).

46 *Macrodema micropterum*
Length, about 3 mm. Widespread throughout Britain on moors, heaths and grey dunes and found under plant litter. With its oblong body and short wings it looks something like a small rove beetle, but is recognizable by its proboscis and antennae with four joints. The adult over-winters and can be found in early spring.

47 *Pionosomus varius*
Length, 2–3 mm. Very restricted in Britain but abundant where located. Found in similar surroundings to the previous species. Hibernating animals can be found under patches of small mouse-ear chickweed. Mating occurs here, also.

48 *Eremocoris abietis*
Length, approx. 7 mm. Not British. A Continental species occurring in sparse coniferous vegetation on sandy soil. Its nymph stage is probably spent in anthills, where it may prey upon the brood, but both nymphs and fully-developed individuals can be found apparently without any association with ants.

49 *Gonianotus marginepunctatus*
Length, 5–5·5 mm. Not common. In Denmark, most frequently found on grey dunes.

50 *Peritrechus geniculatus*
Length, 5–6 mm. Common in Britain on dry sandy soil among fallen leaves and short vegetation, at times in great numbers; also on chalk in the south-east. The nymphs, which are seen in summer, are easily recognized by their brown colour and black longitudinal stripes.

51 *Rhyparochromus pini*
Length, 7–8 mm. Found in most counties south of the English

midlands. A large and beautiful groundbug which is common on sandy soil, particularly under fallen bark or other pine litter. Hibernating animals can often be found in autumn, in small groups, under loose bark on dry branches and in similar places.

52 *Alydus calcaratus*
Length, 11–12 mm. This bug requires dry, sandy heaths. The Bagshot district is the classical British environment. It also occurs on moors and similar places, where it scuttles about among the low plants or sits in the higher vegetation. Unlike most terrestrial bugs, it is an excellent flier. The upper side of the abdomen is bright orange-red, so that in flight the bug looks like the spider-hunting wasp, *Pompilus* (215). The nymphs closely resemble ants (see also 22 and 31) and are found in the nests of various species of ant. Not much is known about the feeding behaviour. Possibly it takes carrion.

53 *Chorosoma schillingi*
Length, 14–16 mm. Confined to coastal dunes in Britain; on the Continent also found inland on basic heaths, etc. Common on marram grass with us. This long thin bug somewhat resembles the tropical and subtropical stick insects. It can be distinguished from 36 by its stouter legs and antennae. The eggs, which are black, oblong and have two projections at one end, can be found in small groups on blades of grass and similar objects. They overwinter and hatch in spring, and the sexually mature animals are seen in July–August.

54 *Arenocoris falleni*
Length, 6–6·5 mm. Largely a southern coastal species in England and Wales, but by no means exclusively maritime on the Continent. Found on sand, often in association with common stork's-bill, which is probably its food plant. The adult over-winters.

55 Juniper Shieldbug, *Pitedia juniperina*
Length, 10–12 mm. Probably now extinct in Britain, where it was at the extreme limit of its range. Found sporadically on juniper, which is its host plant. Shieldbugs (55–60) can be distinguished from other bugs by their plump body and their antennae with five joints. All the shieldbugs mentioned here over-winter as adults.

56 *Rhacognathus punctatus*
Length, 7–10 mm. Occurs sparingly throughout Britain in the damper parts of heaths. Unlike most shieldbugs this species is predatory, feeding on, among other prey, the leaf beetle *Lochmaea suturalis* (197). The example illustrated is brighter green than is usually the case in this species.

57 Bishop's Mitre, *Aelia acuminata*

Length, 8–9 mm. Very common on tall and rank grasses in widely different places south of a line from Norfolk to Cornwall. It can become a pest on wheat, but readily takes the juices of other grasses, like marram. Many of the hibernating animals are killed by fungi. The nymphs, which hatch in early summer, have a more oval shape than the adults.

58 *Podops inuncta*

Length, 5–6 mm. Common in England south of Norfolk, but often overlooked. Over-winters in dry places at the bottom of grass tufts. Later in the year can be found in damper places. Its feeding habits are not known. It has been found near manure, but whether or not this means that it is saprophagous remains uncertain.

59 *Sciocoris cursitans*

Length, approx. 5 mm. Often abundant in southern England. Occurs on the ground in dry, warm localities on sand or chalk. Its food plants are not known. Males stridulate.

60 *Legnotus picipes*

Length, 3–4 mm. Occurs in all the south coast counties of England, as well as in East Anglia and the Midlands. It can be seen on moors and grey dunes often under species of bedstraw.

HEMIPTERA-HOMOPTERA: Plant Bugs

61 *Cixius similis*

Length, 4–5 mm. In Denmark, mainly found on the poorer and lighter soils of Jutland. Seen on the wing throughout the summer.

62 *Ommatidiotus dissimilis*

Length, 4–5 mm. Easily recognized by a dark stripe on the middle of its head and on the front part of its body. The illustrated example is a female, but most females are more short-winged. The male is smaller with a black edge to the wings. In Denmark it is confined to Jutland, where it can be seen on moorland in July–August.

63 *Neophilaenus pallidus*

Lengths, male approx. 5·5 mm, female approx. 6·5 mm. A close relative of the froghopper, and one of the commonest insects in the dunes. It has only recently been distinguished from the equally common species *N. lineatus*. It is bigger than the latter, has paler colours, and appears to be mainly found in the marram grass vegetation of the dunes, whereas *lineatus* can be found on reed and sedge in bogs and wet meadows.

64 *Idiocerus lituratus*

Length, 6–6·5 mm. Found in July–September on willow, including creeping willow in dunes. Common all over the country.

65 *Ulopa reticulata*
Length, 3-4 mm. Common throughout the summer on dry moors, where it can be found around the basal parts of plants. In Denmark, it is normally long-winged like the two illustrated examples, but in the rest of Scandinavia it is always short-winged. The long-winged form has posterior wings, which the short-winged type lacks.

66 *Psammotettix exilis*
Length, approx. 3 mm. Belongs to a genus comprising many species difficult to distinguish from each other. This one colonizes dry places more than do others in the genus and can be found on dunes with lyme grass vegetation.

67 *Macropsis impura*
Length, 3-4 mm. Widespread in sandy areas over the whole country. Found on creeping willow and seen in July–August.

68 *Mocuellus collinus*
Length, approx. 4 mm. Common and found widespread over the whole country. Found, among other places, on dunes with lyme grass vegetation.

69 *Euscelis plebeius*
Length, approx. 4·5 mm. Found from May to September in rather varied habitats. Frequently seen on dunes. The species can be recognized by the numerous black spots on its head and body.

NEUROPTERA: Lacewings

70 **Ant-lion,** *Myrmeleon formicarius*
Wing length, approx. 35 mm. Not British. The ant-lion frequents sandy areas which are sunny but protected from the wind as, for instance, those on dunes, rides and fire-breaks in dune plantations. There are two species in Denmark, but they only occur in a few places, on Bornholm, in north Zealand (Tisvilde), south Falster and Skagen and on Laesø. Adult ant-lions are seldom seen. They mature in June–July, but hide in vegetation during the day and fly at dusk. The funnel-shaped snares of the larvae are frequently seen in the sand (70b). The funnel, 3-4 cm in diameter and two centimetres deep, is dug by the larva (70a), which sits concealed at the bottom with only its sharply pointed mandibles protruding. Small animals, e.g. ants, falling into the funnel are seized by the mandibles and their body fluids sucked out. Grains of sand, which fall down on to the head of the ant-lion, produce a reflex causing the larva to bombard its surroundings with the grains. In the autumn the larva buries itself deeper in the ground and spins a cocoon. It pupates after hibernating, and the adult ant-lion emerges in June–July.

71 Green Lacewing, *Chrysopa abbreviata*

Wing length, approx. 12 mm. Green lacewings as a group are generally familiar as they often come into houses to hibernate. In spring they leave when about to lay their eggs. These are deposited in groups on the underside of leaves and are attached to the end of a thread 5 mm long. The thread is made when the female secretes a drop of slime on the leaf. She then lifts her abdomen, and the slime is pulled out into a filament which hardens in the air and the egg is extruded at the end of this. The species illustrated is common on dunes. Both the adult and the larva (71a) feed on aphids. The larva crawls about over leaves and sucks the blood of aphids one at a time.

MICROLEPIDOPTERA: 'Small' Moths

72 Large Bagworm, *Pachytelia villosella*

Wing length, 10–12 mm. The larva of this species lives in a bag (72a) built from straw and twig spun together. As the larva grows new material is added to the bag. The species is found on both heather and broom, but in Denmark only occurs in those parts of Jutland where heather grows. The larva takes two years to develop. Before pupation in the middle of May the bag is spun together. There is a marked difference between the male and the female. The male is winged and 'normal', whereas the female is wingless and, furthermore, lacks legs, eyes, mouth and antennae. She remains partly inside the bag after emergence and is visited here by the male, when mating takes place.

73 Broom Moth, *Leucoptera spartifoliella*

Wing length, 3–4 mm. The species is found on the broom which grows in many places on dunes. The larva mines the bark. The delicate-looking moths are about at dusk and resemble small white pieces of fluff on the food plant.

74 Sac Moth, *Coleophora bilineatella*

Wing length, 6–7 mm. Like the previous species, found on broom. The larva feeds on the leaves and makes its cocoon of leaves spun together, and it pupates later in this cocoon (74a). The sacs are often established on blades of grass next to broom.

75 *Lobesia littoralis*

Wing length, 6–7 mm. Like 77 this species is a leaf-roller. Found in sandy places all over the country, but mainly near coasts. It has two generations; the first flies in the latter half of May and in June, the second in the latter half of July and in August. The larva lives on the shoots, leaves and flowers of thrift.

76 *Swamerdamia conspersella*
Wing length, 7–8 mm. One of the small ermine moths. The larva lives on crowberry and the adult flies at dusk over the plants. Very localized.

77 *Argyroploce arbutella*
Wing length, 6–7 mm. This beautiful small moth is one of the leaf-rollers and in Denmark is only found in Jutland. It has two generations in a year, one in May–June, the other in July–August. The larva feeds on bearberry.

78 *Gymnancycla canella*
Wing length, 8–10 mm. Its basic colour varies considerably from white-grey and yellow shades to light brick-red. The coloration makes it almost impossible to see when it is at rest on the sand. The larva lives on saltwort.

79 **Grass Moth,** *Catoptria fulgidella*
Wing length, 11–13 mm. Found in drier and more sandy places than most of our numerous other species of grass moths. It can be seen in all parts of the country and occurs in August. The larva feeds on roots of sedges.

80 *Melissoblaptes zelleri*
Wing length, 10–16 mm. Found in the damper parts of dunes, where the female can be seen taking short flights in calm, warm evenings during July–August. The males sit on the sand or in the vegetation and vibrate their wings intermittently. These signals apparently serve to attract the female. The larva feeds on moss and lives in the sand in a burrow several centimetres deep.

81 *Selagia spadicella*
Wing length, 12–14 mm. Found in July–August in heather-covered places: it is, however, only seen in a few areas. The larva lives under the heather plants in silk-lined burrows in the sand. The colour is reddish-white with red lines on the back and a few olive-green spots.

82 *Hysterosia hilarana*
Wing length, 8–10·5 mm. Seen from the middle of July until the middle of August. The larva lives in a stem gall on field wormwood and pupates inside this.

83 *Titanio pollinalis*
Wing length, 8–9 mm. In Denmark, a species found only in Jutland, where it occurs in great numbers in certain localities. The adult flies during the day in the sunshine and can be seen in May–June. The larva is light grey with five greyish-brown longitudinal stripes, black warts and black head and neck-shield and it is seen in July–August in a tubular web on broom, needle furze, etc. Pupation takes place inside the web.

LEPIDOPTERA:
Clearwing Moths

84 Thrift Clearwing, *Aegeria*
(= Sesia) muscaeformis
Wing length, 5–6 mm. The
smallest species of clearwing in
Britain. The larva develops in one
year and lives on the root of thrift.
Moths can be caught in June–
August in regions near the coast
where large colonies of the food
plant occur. A better method of
obtaining the moth is to gather
the plants attacked by the larvae in
May–June and rear them in
captivity.

LEPIDOPTERA:
Geometrid Moths

85 European Emerald, *Thalera*
fimbrialis
Wing length, 15–17 mm. A central
European geometrid, known in
England only as a rare straggler.
In Denmark, found exclusively
near the coasts, but without being
directly connected with the beach
or dunes. Occurs sporadically.
The larva lives on thyme, milfoil,
wormwood, heather and other
plants growing in fairly dry places.
It hibernates and can be seen
especially in May–June on the
food plants. The moth flies from
the middle of July to the middle of
August.

86 *Rhodostrophia vibicaria*
Wing length, 14–16 mm. The
colour varies considerably; in
Denmark individuals from the
west coast of Jutland are on the
whole more reddish than individuals from other parts of the
country. Like the previous species
this one is found near the coasts.
It is not, however, wholly dependent on maritime situations
but is associated with dry, grass-
covered places, moors, etc., where
its food plants, broom, needle
furze, heather, etc., are established.
The larva is long and thin. It
over-winters, and the moth flies
from the middle of June to the
end of July.

87 *Lythria purpurata*
Wing length, 11–15 mm. Long
reported as a British insect, but
records of its capture are un-
convincing. The larva feeds on
sheep's sorrel in sandy, sunny
places. The two generations are on
the wing from June to the middle
of August. The moth is very
active by day, flying low over the
ground for short distances, and is
found in suitable places all over
the country. The larva is easily
recognized by its red back and
green underside.

88 *Ortholitha plumbaria*
Wing length, 16–19 mm. This and
the closely related British species,
the lead belle (*O. mucronata*), are
both common on the moors of
Jutland. The latter flies in May
and in the beginning of June,
whereas *plumbaria* is seen from late

June till the middle of August. The larvae of both species live on needle furze, broom and heather.

89 Narrow-winged Pug,
Eupithecia nanata
There are about 50 species of *Eupithecia* in north-west Europe. These are small geometrid moths with a wing length of about 8–12 mm and many of them have very similar markings and coloration. Most are associated with one particular plant genus on which the larva lives. The present species feeds on heather and is widespread and common on moors. It has two generations which fly from May till August. Larva, 119.

90 Grass Wave, *Perconia strigillaria*
Wing length, 15–17 mm. Its coloration varies considerably, especially with regard to the number, width and position of the dark lines. It occurs on most of the heaths and moors throughout southern Britain. Flies from late May till the middle of July. The larva, 25–30 mm long, over-winters and in spring feeds on heather and, in rarer cases, on broom and needle furze. It is easily recognized by the projections on its back. It is grey with a yellow lateral stripe and a black back-stripe along which there are brown stripes.

91 Netted Mountain Moth,
Isturgia carbonaria
Wing length, 9–12 mm. In Britain, confined to certain Scottish mountains. The larva of this species lives exclusively on bearberry. The moth flies readily in sunshine in the middle of the day and is on the wing in May and at the beginning of June. The larva lives on the underside of the leaves. It is green with a crimson patch at the end of the abdomen. Over-winters as a pupa.

92 Bordered Grey,
Selidosema ericetaria
Wing length, 12–17 mm. Very local in Britain, where it occurs on heaths and mosses. It flies from the middle of July till the middle of August and is very lively on warm days. The larva lives on heather, broom, restharrow and clover, as well as on other plants. It over-winters while young and can be netted in spring on its food plants.

93 Common Heath, *Ematurga atomaria*
Wing length, 12–16 mm. Abundant on practically every heath in the British Isles. The moth flies in two generations from May till August, and it is the pupae of the second generation which over-winter. Distinctly a diurnal species. There is a considerable difference between the appearance of the female (93) and that of the male (93a). Larva, 120.

94 Annulet, *Gnophos obscurata*
Wing length, 20–22 mm. Mainly a maritime species in Britain. It occurs on moors as well as along old stone walls near woods or on dry slopes. It flies from the middle of July till the middle of August. The larva lives on various plants like wormwood, dock, goosefoot and stonecrop. It is short and fat and over-winters when half-grown: it becomes fully-grown in the following May.

95 Streak, *Chesias legatella*
Wing length, 16–18 mm. Widespread over the whole of Britain. The moth flies late in the year, from the middle of September to late October. The eggs over-winter and the green or yellowish larvae are seen in May on broom.

LEPIDOPTERA:
Zygaenid Moths

96 Transparent Burnet,
Zygaena purpuralis
Wing length, approx. 9 mm. Locally common in the British Isles. Easily distinguished from other burnet moths found in this country by the two merging red spots on the elytra. There are, however, two closely related forms with the same wing coloration. Whereas the adults of these are difficult to distinguish, the larvae are very different and live on different host plants. The larva of the typical *purpuralis* is yellow and feeds on thyme, whereas the

larva of the other form is whitish-grey and lives on pimpernel. The type illustrated flies in late June and July and can be seen all over the country, although it only occurs sporadically.

LEPIDOPTERA:
Hawk Moths

97 Bedstraw Hawk, *Celerio*
(=*Deilephila*) *galii*
Wing length, 30–40 mm. A migrant which periodically invades Britain in numbers. It flies in warm evenings after sunset and visits a number of different kinds of flowers from the beginning of June to the middle of August to suck nectar. The frequency of the species varies considerably; in some years it is very numerous, but in others only a few are reported. Larva, 122.

LEPIDOPTERA:
Moths with Spinning Larvae

98 Puss Moth, *Dicranura vinula*
Wing length, 25–34 mm. On the wing in May, June and July. The species is common all over Britain, but appears to thrive best on light soil. It can be found even on sand dunes. It is associated with such trees as willow, poplar and aspen, including the dwarf willows of dunes. Larva, 123.

99 Dark Tussock, *Dasychira*
fascelina
Wing length, 16–23 mm. Chiefly a northern insect in Britain. Flies

from the middle of June till the beginning of August. Like the previous species, often seen mating, at rest on telephone poles. Larva, 124.

100 Oak Eggar, *Lasiocampa quercus*

Wing length, 25–35 mm. The female (100a) is bigger and paler than the male. The appearance of the species can vary considerably. Found all over Britain but most frequently on light soils. The moth flies in July and in the first half of August. The males fly in the afternoon in full sunlight with a pronounced zigzag flight. Mating takes place by day. The female deposits her eggs during flight among willow and bog myrtle. Larva, 126.

101 Pebble Prominent, *Notodonta ziczac*

Wing length, approx. 22 mm. A common and widely distributed moth which can be seen in willow-marshes and willow-scrubs and in the aspen-scrubs of the moors, as well as on poplars. The moth is noticed during the day sitting exposed on branches and tree-trunks. Larva, 127.

102 Heath Vapourer, *Orgyia ericae*

Wing length, approx. 10 mm. The cocoons (102b) of this moth can be seen at the end of July and in August fixed to the tops of heather plants. The moth flies in August and September. Only the male has functional wings. The female (102a) is flightless and remains in the cocoon. After mating is effected, the fertilized eggs over-winter in the body of the dead female. A widespread species in the moorland areas of central and western Jutland. It also occurs in other parts of the country and in Britain. Larva, 125.

103 Emperor Moth, *Saturnia pavonia*

Wing length, 30–36 mm. The female (103a) is bigger and greyer than the male. The latter has feathery antennae, like the males of most of the silk-moths. These antennae carry the olfactory organs which receive the scents of the female: by them the male can locate the female over long distances. The moth flies from the end of April to the middle of June: males fly during the day, females only at night. The species can be found all over Britain, but is commonest on moors and other places with light soil. Larva, 128.

LEPIDOPTERA: Noctuid Moths

104 Archer's Dart, *Agrotis vestigialis*

Wing length, 15–17 mm. The forewings have a distinct marking, the shade of which can vary considerably. The females are often darker than the males. The size can vary. The species is found in great

74

numbers in sandy places, for
instance in many coastal areas, and
is commonest on the eastern and
southern coasts of Britain and in
Cheshire, Lancashire and Yorkshire. Flies in July–August, and
the species is often seen on the
wing during the day. The larva
lives in the ground, where it feeds
on grass roots.

105 True Lover's Knot,
Lycophotia porphyrea
Wing length, 13–14 mm. The
species is found in heather-covered
places. Widespread on commons,
heaths and moorlands throughout
Britain. Its colour can vary considerably, and individuals from the
eastern part of Denmark are often
more reddish than those found in
Jutland. It flies from late June till
late August. The moth is often
seen during the day. The larva,
which feeds on heather, over-
winters in the penultimate instar.

**106 Beautiful Yellow
Underwing,** *Anarta
myrtilli*
Wing length, 10–12 mm. This
small and attractive noctuid is
common in places where heather
grows. The colour of the forewings
resembles that of heather flowers.
The moth flies during the day and
visits the flowers of bilberry, cran-
berry, bearberry, bell-heather and
heather. It has a rapid, steady
flight. There are two generations
overlapping each other and the

moth can be seen from May till
late August. Larva, 121.

107 *Oligia literosa*
Wing length, 11–12 mm. As in the
case of 110 there are two varieties
of this species in Denmark. On the
west coast from Skagen to Rømø
(and farther on to the coast of
Holland) the sandy-coloured variety, *onychina*, can be found. This
often has a bluish tint and lacks
markings. The type, *O. literosa*
(107a), is found on the coasts in
all other parts of the country and
in some cases also in inland places.
The moth flies from the middle of
July to the middle of August. The
larvae live in the stems of lyme and
other grasses.

108 *Hyphilare littoralis*
Wing length, approx. 16 mm. This
noctuid is a typical dune species.
Flies in July, when it swarms in
lyme grass in great numbers and
visits the flowers of this plant. Its
larvae can be seen during the day
in the sand by the roots of lyme;
at night they move up into the
green parts of the plant to feed.

**109 Lesser Yellow
Underwing,** *Triphaena
comes*
Wing length, 16–18 mm. A close
relative of the common yellow
underwing, *T. pronuba* (*Woodland
Life*, Nos. 118 and 198). Found
throughout Britain and is on the
wing from about the first week of

July to the beginning of September, when it can be seen on light soil, such as that of dunes. The larva is brownish with a broad, white back-line and diamond-shaped back spots. Feeds on various grasses.

110 *Apamea (= Hadena) sordida engelharti*
Wing length, 14–18 mm. This insect is only found on the west coast of Jutland and on the North Frisian Islands. Like 107 it must be regarded as an ecological variety of a more widespread main species. The type, *A. sordida sordida*, is found over the whole of Denmark, but is not common. The west coast variety, *engelharti*, varies in appearance, like the main species, but is always more sand-grey. It flies from the middle of June till the end of July. The larva lives on grass roots and overwinters when half-grown.

111 Lyme Grass, *Arenostola elymi*
Wing length, 15–17 mm. Typical of yellow dunes, where it is associated with lyme grass. The larva lives inside the stems and pupates at the bottom of these or in the sand near by. The moth flies from the middle of June till the middle of August. In the evenings it visits the flowers of lyme grass. An east-coast species in Britain.

112 Coast Dart, *Euxoa cursoria*
Wing length, 14–16 mm. The coloration can vary considerably and three different colour forms are shown in the plate. A local species in Britain, occurring on coastal sandhills. Flies from the middle of July till the middle of September and the moth visits heather flowers and flowering grasses. The larva lives in sand near the roots of its food plants.

LEPIDOPTERA: Butterflies

113 *Maculinea alcon*
Wing length, 17–19 mm. Not British. In Denmark, confined to Jutland, where the butterfly is to be seen in July–August in the dunes. The female (113a) is much darker than the male. The larva lives on gentian and its development is like that of the following species.

114 Large Blue, *Maculinea arion*
Wing length, 17–21 mm. A rare English Lycaenid and the biggest of our blues. Found on light soils and in sandy areas, where it is about in July–August. Its flight is rather heavy and as a butterfly it is wary. The number of spots on the top side varies. It deposits eggs on the flowers of thyme growing near anthills. After the larva has lived for some time on the flowers, the ants bring the larva into their nest, where it overwinters and eats ant larvae. The larva has a nectar gland, the secretion of which is taken by the adult ants.

115 *Fabriciana* (=*Argynnis*) *niobe*
Wing length, 21–25 mm. The actual occurrence of this fritillary in England is exceedingly doubtful. The species flies in July–August and is found on poor soil. It is often seen on dunes and is known from all parts of Denmark. The eggs are deposited on moss and over-winter. The larva appears in April and lives on violets: it is approx. 40 mm long and is brown with pink spines, a white line on its back and a white triangle on each of its sections. It pupates in June and the adult butterfly appears shortly after.

116 Queen of Spain Fritillary,
Argynnis (=*Issoria*) *lathonia*
Wing length, 20–23 mm. In England, a butterfly mainly of the south-east and a migrant from the Continent. The pearly spots on the underside of the hind wings are large—see 116a. Has two generations in a year. The spring generation flies in May–June, the summer brood in July–September. The flight is rapid but the butterfly is often seen sitting on the ground in the sun. The larva feeds on species of violet and pupates on the food plant.

117 Grayling, *Satyrus*
(=*Hipparchia*) *semele*
Wing length, 24–28 mm. One of the commonest butterflies found on dunes. Its flight is fast and vigorous. It often sits on the sand

and stays absolutely still after landing. It rests with its wings folded vertically, when the brownish, mottled underside of the hind pair makes the insect almost unnoticeable. The flying period is July–August and the species occurs all over the country. It has a mating display in which the male performs a tripping dance to the female. The pale spots are smaller in the male (117a) than in the female. Larva, 129.

118 Wall butterfly, *Pararge*
(=*Lasiommata*) *megera*
Wing length, 19–23 mm. It frequents warm, dry, sunny situations and is often seen on grass-covered beach ridges and in grey dunes. The first generation flies in May–June, the second generation in August–September. The number of butterflies varies considerably from year to year and from place to place. The species is probably declining in Britain although generally common still. The bluish green larva, which has three pale lines on the sides, feeds on various grasses.

**LEPIDOPTERA:
Larvae of Moths and Butterflies**

119 Narrow-winged Pug,
Eupithecia nanata
Length, to 12 mm. Lives on heather. The larvae of the first generation are often greenish, like the leaves of the heather plant,

whereas those of the second generation are whitish with arrow-shaped spots of the same red colour as the flowers of the heather. Imago, 89.

120 Common Heath, *Ematurga atomaria*

Length, to 22 mm. Although often seen on heather, it is not closely associated with this plant. The larva is usually seen from the middle of September. Imago, 93.

121 Beautiful Yellow Underwing, *Anarta myrtilli*

Length, to 30 mm. It lives mainly on heather, but can also be observed on other plants. The first generation of larvae is seen in July, the second from the end of August. Imago, 106.

122 Bedstraw Hawk, *Celerio* (=*Deilephila*) *galii*

Length, to 80 mm. Lives in the bedstraw vegetation of the dunes and can at times be seen in some numbers, usually in July. The pupae over-winter. The appearance of the larva varies considerably. Imago, 97.

123 Puss Moth, *Dicranura vinula*

Length, 70–80 mm. Feeds in late summer on willow, poplar and aspen. When touched it takes up a threatening attitude, shooting the long, red threads of its two tail tubes out and drawing its head into the first thoracic segment. Pupates in autumn and spins a cocoon in the bark. Pieces of the bark are incorporated in the cocoon, so that this becomes hard and stiff. It over-winters in this cocoon. Imago. 98,

124 Dark Tussock, *Dasychira fascelina*

Length, to 35 mm. The larva is found on a number of different plants, for instance broom, heather and creeping willow. The young larva over-winters and pupates in May–June when it is fully-grown, having eaten throughout spring. A larva easily recognized by the combination of white and black hairs on its dorsal brushes. Imago, 99.

125 Heath Vapourer, *Orgyia ericae*

Length, to 20 mm. In spring the young larvae hatch from eggs retained in the abdomen of the dead mother. They feed on the new, fresh shoots of heather, bell-heather and bog myrtle and are fully-developed in July. Then they spin cocoons in the tops of plants. Imago, 102.

126 Oak Eggar, *Lasiocampa quercus*

Length, up to 70 mm. The name is somewhat unfortunate as the larva probably never feeds on oak, although it occurs on many different plants. The young larva over-winters and is fully-grown in May–June, when it pupates in a cocoon (126a). Imago, 100.

127 Pebble Prominent
Notodonta ziczac
Length, up to 40 mm. This characteristic larva is frequently seen on the leaves of aspen and willow, both of which often form scrub on moors; and in the hollows of dunes. Imago, 101.

128 Emperor Moth, *Saturnia pavonia*
Length, up to 60 mm. The colour varies considerably, but is usually greenish. A transverse row of warts with stiff brushes is found on each segment. The larva occurs on various plants, frequently on heather for instance. It is fully-grown in August. Before pupation it spins a pear-shaped cocoon (128b): the pupa over-winters in the lower part of heather plants. Imago, 103.

129 Grayling, *Satyrus* (= *Hipparchia*) *semele*
Length, up to 30 mm. This larva, which has longitudinal stripes, lives on grasses. Over-winters when young and reaches full size in the following spring. The short pupation period in June–July is spent in a hollow in the ground. Imago, 117.

COLEOPTERA: Carnivorous Beetles and Ground Beetles

130 Wood Tiger Beetle,
Cicindela sylvatica
Length, 15–19 mm. Tiger beetles are predatory forms which attack other insects. The present species feeds mainly on ants. It is widely distributed, but local in Britain. It can be seen in May–June and in August and less frequently in July. Notwithstanding its popular name, it is found chiefly on sandy heaths.

131 Brown Tiger Beetle,
Cicindela hybrida
Length, 12–16 mm. It includes *C. maritimum*, now considered to be a subspecies of *hybrida*. Rather local, like the previous species, and one usually seen in sand and gravel areas exposed to the sun, e.g. beaches, dunes and heaths. Overwintered individuals are found in May–June and the newly hatched insects in August–September. Buries itself in sand at night. When the temperature of the sand is around 30°C, it is able to fly in short, low arcs. Feeds on other insects, which are caught by running and jumping. Larva, 192.

132 *Carabus arvensis*
Length, 16–18 mm. This ground beetle is somewhat smaller than the very common species *C. nemoralis* (*Field and Meadow Life*, No. 221); both have furrowed indentations on the elytra. Especially common on the poorer, sandy soils of Jutland. Most numerous in May. Larva, 193.

133 *Carabus nitens*
Length, 13–16 mm. The smallest and handsomest member of its genus. Distinguished from the other species of *Carabus* found in

Britain by its green colour and by the fact that the points of its front tibia are elongated in the shape of a tooth. Widespread but not common. Can be seen on open, heather-covered soil. Most numerous in early summer; rarer in August–September.

134 *Notiophilus aquaticus*
Length, 4·5–6 mm. Easily recognized by its shape, which is of uniform width, and by its large eyes. A fairly common beetle on open, slightly damp gravel, and is known in all parts of the country. Most numerous in July–August. Two varieties occur in Britain.

135 *Elaphrus riparius*
Length, 6·5–7·5 mm. A common British species known by its characteristic shape and coloration. Mainly seen in June in damp, sunny places with gravel and sand, which are more or less bare of vegetation.

136 *Dyschirius obscurus*
Length, 3·5–4·5 mm. A small ground beetle found on the firm, bare stretches of fine sand near coasts. It lives here together with the rove beetle, *Bledius arenarius* (147), the larvae and pupae of which are its main food. A good digger, it is only seen for short periods in the sunshine on the actual surface of the sand. The adult over-winters and is most abundant in May–June.

137 *Broscus cephalotes*
Length, 17–22 mm. Found on fairly varied soil, in dunes among other places. It digs a deep burrow and lurks at the opening waiting for prey. It also searches for prey on the surface of the sand at night. If dug out of the sand during the day, it takes up a peculiar position, feigning death, with mandibles and legs extended. Many desert animals have similar behaviour. The beetle, found from May to September, is common throughout Britain.

138 *Harpalus smaragdinus*
Length, 9–11 mm. Widely distributed but not common. It frequents dry and open sandy soil, and is most abundant in May–June. The species has two generations; one reproduces in autumn, the larva over-wintering, and the other over-winters as adult and reproduces in spring.

139 *Harpalus rubripes*
Length, 9–11 mm. Can be seen in the same places as the previous species from April to October. Adults as well as larvae over-winter.

140 *Bradycellus harpalinus*
Length, 3·8–4·5 mm. A common ground beetle on open sandy soil and gravel near the roots of heather. Most abundant in August, when it can be netted on vegetation in the evening.

141 *Amara spreta*
Length, 7–8·5 mm. The genus *Amara* comprises about 30 species in north-west Europe, many of which are common. This particular species, although not common, is characteristic of dry and open sandy soil with little vegetation, such as that of dunes. Mainly seen in May–July.

142 *Amara bifrons*
Length, 5·7–6·8 mm. Widely distributed but not common. Like the previous form prefers sunny, open, sandy soil: it can also be seen on plants. Found from May–September, but its greatest numbers are in July–August. The larva over-winters.

143 *Calathus mollis*
Length, 6–9 mm. Found on dry, sandy stretches exposed to the sun, preferably near the beach and in dunes, where it lives near the roots of plants like lyme grass. Most frequently seen in July–August.

144 *Dromius linearis*
Length, 4·3–5·2 mm. A very common British beetle. This slim, pale-coloured insect is to be seen in dunes near the roots of lyme and marram grass. It can be netted on the plants in the evening. The adult over-winters and can be seen nearly the whole year.

145 *Metabletus truncatellus*
Length 2·6–3·4 mm. Uncommon. Found where the soil is dry and sunny.

146 *Pterostichus punctulatus*
Length, 11–14 mm. The genus *Pterostichus* comprises some of our commonest ground beetles, among them *P. melanarius*, which is frequently found in cellars. The species illustrated here is not common, but occurs on dry, sandy moorland soil and on gravel.

COLEOPTERA:
Rove Beetles ('Staphs')
147 *Bledius arenarius*
Length, 3–3·5 mm. Beetles of the genus *Bledius* share with but few other coleopterans the rare distinction of being gregarious in habit. All live in burrows, which they dig in clay or sand. There can be up to 2000 individuals per square metre. This species lives on bare, damp, sandy soil near the coasts. It digs a vertical Y-shaped burrow and feeds on microscopic algae, which it scrapes off the sand grains. In the burrows its larvae are eaten by the ground beetle *Dyschirius obscurus* (136). Other *Bledius* species can be found in yellow and grey dunes.

148 *Stenus geniculatus*
Length, 3·8–4·5 mm. Widely distributed but not common. Found mainly on moorland hills under heather, moss and lichen. Like other species of *Stenus* it is a predatory animal feeding on springtails; it catches its prey by quickly extruding its long tongue which has an adhesive tip.

149 *Philonthus varians*
Length, 5–7 mm. It is one of the few of our 49 species of *Philonthus* with red coloration on the elytra. A common rove beetle in fairly varied habitats, including moorland hills where it lurks under heather and lichen, and on beaches under seaweed. Found in May–October.

150 *Creophilus maxillosus*
Length, 15–22 mm. The single British representative of the genus. Common all over the country. Can be seen in May–October on carrion, dung and rotting plants.

151 **Devil's Coach-Horse,**
Ocypus (=Staphylinus) olens
Length, 24–30 mm. Our longest rove beetle. Found both in woods and on open soil, on moors and on dunes. Active in May–September.

COLEOPTERA:
Burying and Rove Beetles

152 **Sexton Beetle,** *Necrophorus interruptus*
Length, 14–18 mm. Sexton (burying) beetles feed on the carcases of birds and small mammals, which they bury and near which they deposit their eggs. They detect carrion from a distance by means of a highly developed sense of smell. The olfactory organs are situated in the antennae, the filaments of which can be spread fan-wise. The species illustrated is closely related to the burying beetle, *N. investigator* (*Woodland Life*, No. 255), but can be distinguished from this by the fact that the foremost of the red transverse bands on the elytra is interrupted in the middle, and that the species has yellow hairs on its hind tibia. Uncommon in England, it is seen in the south mainly on sandy soil. Larva, 194.

153 *Saprinus semistriatus*
Length, 3·5–6 mm. Most abundant in May–August and lives on sandy soil on carrion, dung and rotting vegetation. Other species of *Saprinus* occur on dunes and beaches.

COLEOPTERA:
Softwings and Click Beetles

154 *Malachius viridis*
Length, 4–5·5 mm. In Britain, occurs only in England, where it is locally distributed. It frequents flowers in June and July. Several species of *Malachius* are found in this country on raised, dry soil, such as that of heathlands and dunes.

155 *Necrobia violacea*
Length, 3·5–4·5 mm. Rather local in Britain, but often numerous where found. Occurs on dry carrion and bones in March–September.

156 *Corymbites aeneus*
Length, 10–16 mm. This click-beetle frequents warm, dry places and is about in June–July. It is

found near grass roots and under stones. The larva, which takes two years to develop, can cause damage to beet and potato crops.

157 *Lacon murinus*
Length, 10–20 mm. Found on open and fairly dry soil and common all over Britain. It can be obtained by sweeping. Seen in May–July and often flies in sunshine. The larva spends much time on the surface of the ground, but eats the roots of plants.

158 *Cryptohypnus pulchellus*
Length, 3–4·5 mm. This beautiful, small click-beetle is found on gravel and sandy soils, particularly those near the coasts, where it can be seen under stones or plant litter or running over the sand. Appears in May–July. Local in distribution.

159 *Dermestes laniarius*
Length, 6·5–8 mm. Closely related to the larder beetle (*D. lardarius*), found as a pest in houses and warehouses where it takes food rich in fat and protein. The present species lives only in the open and can be seen on sandy soil on carrion and bones or under heather and stones. Appears mainly in early and late summer.

160 *Orthocerus clavicornis*
Length, 3·2–5 mm. Is easily recognized by its peculiar antennae. The species is fairly common in sandy areas. It can be dis-

covered under mosses and lichens in May–August.

161 *Heterocerus fusculus*
Length, 3–3·6 mm. Like 136 and 147 it is a burrowing beetle, living on sandy plains and dunes. If anyone steps on the spots where the small hills from their burrowing betray the presence of the beetles, or if water is poured over these hills, the animals will appear on the surface. The species also excavates in mud by fresh water on moorland.

162 *Byrrhus pilula*
Length, 7·5–11 mm. Common all over Britain at the roots of grasses, in mosses, etc. on sandy soil, and often noticed wandering over paths. Seen most frequently in early summer. Over-winters as the imago.

COLEOPTERA: Ladybirds
163 Eleven-spot Ladybird,
Coccinella undecimpunctata
Length, 3·5–5 mm. Reminiscent of a common seven-spot ladybird, *C. septempunctata* (*Field and Meadow Life*, No. 289), with four additional spots. Mainly found near the beach and common all over the country. Both the larva and the imago can be seen crawling around on plants infested with aphids. Larva, 196.

164 *Coccinella hieroglyphia*
Length, 3·5–4·5 mm. A widespread but not very common

species which is mainly found on moorland soil and in heather bogs. It can be netted on heather and other moorland plants. Remarkably variable in its colour pattern.

165 Sixteen-spot Ladybird, *Tytthaspis sedecimpunctata*
Length, 2·5–3 mm. A fairly common species on sandy soil and gravel, especially near beaches. To be seen in March–May and again in July–October. Found generally over the country.

COLEOPTERA:
Oil Beetles and Nocturnal Ground Beetles

166 *Notoxus monocerus*
Length, 4–4·5 mm. Local in England and Scotland on gravel and sandy soil, both coastal and inland. It can be seen near plant roots or running about in the open and can also be netted. Appears in May–October. The larva is found in the same places.

167 Oil Beetle, *Meloë variegatus*
Length, 11·38 mm. Very rare in Britain, records of it being restricted to Hampshire and Kent. Oil beetles are seen in spring and early summer crawling around on the ground in the sunshine, especially in the morning. Found on sandy commons, moors, dunes and other waste places. They lack hind wings. The female digs several hollows in the soil, in each of

which she deposits up to a thousand eggs. Larva, 195.

168 *Lagria hirta*
Length, 7–10 mm. Although only local in Britain, often numerous, where found. This beetle, which is covered with thick golden hair, commonly appears in July–October, the peak being attained in July–August. It lives on fairly dry soil and can be netted in the vegetation. The larva lives under plant litter on the ground: it overwinters and pupates in spring.

169 *Isomira murina*
Length, 4·5–5·5 mm. Found on sunny gravel and sandy soil in June–July and common all over the country.

170 *Crypticus quisquilius*
Length, 6–7 mm. Our only species of *Crypticus*, local but widespread from Yorkshire southwards and in places in Ireland. Frequents moorland and sandy soil, where it can be seen next to plant roots, under stones and in similar places, mainly in May–August. The larva lives in the same places.

171 *Phylan gibbus*
Length, 7·5–8·5 mm. Again our only species of the genus, widely distributed but local. This and the following species are typical dune animals, as they need high temperatures to be active, and tolerate low humidity and strong light. Nocturnal ground beetles are the

forms most frequently found in hot deserts. The present species is a sluggish animal which can go without food for a considerable time and which devours dry plant material. The larva lives in the sand and is also herbivorous. Active in May–August.

172 *Melanimon tibialis*
Length, 3–4 mm. Generally distributed in Britain. Like the previous species colonizes gravel and sandy soil covered by vegetation: often to be seen in great numbers in hot, dry summers. Active in May–June. Like other beetles of its kind it has a thick and hard exoskeleton. It is thought that this serves as protection against ultra-violet light. The larva feeds on lichens, among other things.

173 *Opatrum sabulosum*
Length, about 10 mm. Restricted in the British Isles to England, south of Lancashire, and to parts of Ireland. Fairly common on open sandy soil, for instance on dunes. It prefers temperatures between 29°C and 34°C. The eggs are deposited on the sand under the leaf-rosettes of cat's-ear and other dune plants, and the imago feeds on the foliage. Larva, 199.

COLEOPTERA: Dung Beetles and Chafers

174 *Copris lunaris*
Length, 17–23 mm. Members of the genus are mainly tropical. In England, *C. lunaris* ranges as far north as Staffordshire. Found in sunny places on hills with sandy soil, but only in a few localities. Seen in May–June. It lives on cow dung: the male and female excavate an oblong burrow in the ground, 15–20 cm under the surface. Here they place 7–8 pear-shaped pellets of dung, on each of which a single egg is deposited.

175 **Bumble-dor,** *Geotrupes vernalis*
Length, 14–20 mm. The English name is more commonly applied to *G. stercorarius*. A fairly plentiful dung beetle in sunny, sandy places. It is found all over Denmark with the exception of Bornholm. Like other dung beetles it digs burrows under lumps of manure. The burrows are filled with dung, and an egg is deposited in each burrow. Dung beetles can 'squeak'. Often in flight in numbers at sunset.

176 **Minotaur Beetle,** *Typhaeus typhoeus*
Length, 15–22 mm. Locally distributed in Britain, occurring in rabbit and sheep dung. Fairly rare now, as habitats suitable for the animals are disappearing. Lives under the dung or at the bottom of burrows, which can go 1–1·5 m into the ground. It swarms in the evening and is most frequently seen in spring, when it mates.

177 Dune Cockchafer,
Anomala (=Euchlora) dubia
Length, 12–15 mm. Locally distributed in Britain on sandy soil,
especially that of dunes. Flies in
June–August, when the males
swarm in the sunshine after the
females, which sit on the sand.
Larva, 198.

178 Cockchafer, *Melontha
hippocastani*
Length, 20–30 mm. Only local in
the British Isles. Very similar to
the common cockchafer *M. melolontha* (*Field and Meadow Life*, No.
304), but has a black line along the
edge of the elytra. The species lives
where there is sandy soil. It takes
four to five years to complete its
metamorphosis in the north but
only three in southern Europe. The
larva feeds on roots and can cause
considerable damage to conifers in
nurseries.

179 *Aphodius foetens*
Length, 6–8 mm. Representative
of the 41 species of *Aphodius* found
in Britain. Fairly common over the
whole country on open sandy soil.
Seen in June–October on cow and
horse dung. The adult over-
winters in the ground.

180 *Aegialia arenaria*
Length, 4–5 mm. Common in
dunes and one of the better known
of our coastline dwellers. Found in
May–July either buried in the
sand at the roots of dune grasses or
moving around on the surface.

**COLEOPTERA: Long-
horned Beetles**

181 Willow Longhorn, *Lamia
textor*
Length, 14–20 mm. Not common,
although distributed both in England and Scotland. It is strange
that this large long-horned beetle
is associated with so insignificant a
plant as creeping willow (*Salix
repens*). This plant grows in grey
dunes and also at the backs of
yellow dunes, as well as on moors.
The beetle appears in summer and
can be seen till September: a slow-
moving insect often seen creeping
over the ground. Larva, 200.

COLEOPTERA: Leaf Beetles

182 *Melasoma collaris*
Length, 5·5–7·5 mm. Found on
sandy soil in dunes and in peat
bogs, and not uncommon. Like the
previous species, lives on creeping
willow. In some summers the
larva can totally defoliate its plant.
There is a row of warts on each
side of its body. When the larva is
irritated, a drop of fluid is extruded from each of these, a secretion
with a strong, unpleasant smell
which tends to repel enemies.

183 *Chrysomela analis*
Length, 3·5–6·5 mm. A widespread
but uncommon leaf beetle, which
can be discovered during the day
under stones and near plant roots
on sandy fields, heathlands, moors
and littoral plains. It comes out

at night and is thought to feed on composites. Found in March–June and again in September.

184 *Lochmaea suturalis*
Length, 5–6 mm. One of the insects most closely associated with heather. Both the adult and the larva eat its leaves. In some years the species occurs in such numbers that heather is destroyed over great areas. Larva, 197.

185 *Cryptocephalus fulvus*
Length, 2–3 mm. Common on sunny, dry soil, where it can be found on low plants, especially in July.

186 *Cassida nebulosa*
Length, 6–8 mm. A rare species of localities in Lincolnshire and southwards. Leaf beetles of this genus are also known as tortoise beetles. *C. nebulosa* is found on plants like goosefoot and orache, and is about in May–September.

COLEOPTERA: Pea 'Weevils' and True Weevils

187 *Bruchidius fasciatus*
Length, 2–3·5 mm. Found on broom and has recently become more abundant. Its eggs are deposited in May–June on the outside of the broom pods. The larvae bore their way into the pod and live in the seeds: both larvae and pupae are to be seen in August–September.

188 *Otiorrhynchus atroapterus*
Length, 7–9 mm. A fairly common weevil locally distributed in dune areas of Britain. The adult is often seen in May–June crawling on the sand and eating the shoots of various plants. The larva lives in the ground, where it feeds on roots. The imago has no hind wings. Most of the 18 British species of *Otiorrhynchus* reproduce parthenogenetically, the eggs developing without fertilization. Consequently there are no males in these species, but this is not the case with the example illustrated here.

189 *Cneorrhinus plagiatus*
Length, 4–9 mm. Not British. Found in Scandinavia on dunes and sandy fields with little vegetation. In early summer, can be seen crawling slowly over the surface. If the ground becomes too hot, it buries itself a couple of centimetres under the sand. In 1948, this weevil suddenly became a pest on vegetables and field crops (cabbages and turnips) in Scandinavia.

190 *Tychius venustus*
Length, 3–3·4 mm. None of the 11 British species of *Tychius* is common. All are to be found in the flowers of papilionaceous plants. The present one occurs on broom, where the larva lives in the pod, causing this to swell.

191 *Cleonus fasciatus*
Length, 7–10 mm. Of very rare

occurrence in Essex and Norfolk, mainly on sandy soil near beaches. The larva feeds inside the root or hypocotyl region of goosefoot and orache. Up to 10 larvae occur together in the swollen underground parts.

COLEOPTERA: Beetle Larvae

192 Brown Tiger Beetle, *Cicindela hybrida*
Length, 12–15 mm. The newly hatched larva digs a vertical burrow which it enlarges gradually. By the time it is fully grown, its excavation is 20–40 cm deep. The strangely shaped larva sits in the opening of the burrow, from where it catches passing insects and spiders. It pulls the prey into the hole and devours it there. If it is disturbed, the occupier falls down into its shaft. Metamorphosis takes two years. *Methoca ichneumonides* (211) is a parasite on this larva. Imago, 131.

193 Ground Beetle, *Carabus arvensis*
Length, 18–20 mm. Larvae of ground beetles have firm exoskeletons and strong legs and mouth parts and live in much the same way as do the adult beetles. The majority are predatory and feed on earthworms, slugs and other small animals. Most ground beetles over-winter as adults. They lay their eggs in spring and the larvae are mainly seen in summer. Imago, 132.

194 Sexton Beetle, *Necrophorus interruptus*
Length, about 25 mm. Larvae of sexton beetles develop in the carcases of small birds and mammals, which the adult beetles had interred before laying their eggs. Pupation takes place in hollows under the carcase or in the walls of the shaft. Imago, 152.

195 Oil Beetle, *Meloë variegatus*
The newly hatched oil beetle larva (195a) is only a couple of millimetres long but very active. It gradually works its way into the corolla of such plants as dandelions. Here it climbs on to any visiting hairy insects like bees and syrphid flies; but only if it happens to reach a species of *Andrena* (256–258), or other solitary bee, does it survive. It leaves the bee again when she reaches her nest in the ground: it becomes sealed in with the bee's egg and eats the store of honey and pollen. After casting its skin several times, it attains a resting stage called the pre-pupa (195). Thereafter follows a second period of feeding, terminated by the true pupal stage. The beetle (167) appears in early spring.

196 Eleven-spot Ladybird, *Coccinella undecimpunctata*
Length, 4–5 mm. Larvae of most ladybirds move around on foliage devouring aphids (greenflies) and are important as aphid controls.

In certain years with hot, dry summers greenflies have ideal conditions for propagation. A corresponding increase in their enemies is then often seen, the enemies including ladybirds, hover flies (289–297) and lacewings (71). Consequently ladybirds often occur in great numbers in late summer. The pupa (196a) is attached to leaves and stems. Imago, 163.

197 Leaf Beetle, *Lochmaea suturalis*

Length, approx. 5 mm. Many leaf beetles are associated with one particular genus of plants or a few closely related forms. This applies to the present species, which feeds only on heather, both as larva and imago. It can cause considerable damage to heather plants. Feeding only takes place at night. Imago, 184.

198 Dune Cockchafer,
  Anomala (= Euchlora) dubia

Length, approx. 30 mm. The C-shaped cockchafer larva is found in the ground, where it devours fine rootlets. The development takes two years: in May–June of its second year it pupates and the adult beetle emerges in July. Imago, 177.

199 Nocturnal Ground Beetle,
  Opatrum sabulosum

Length, approx. 15 mm. Like the previous species it lives on the roots

of various dune plants, but can tolerate dry conditions better than the larva of the dune cockchafer. This may be owing to a thicker and more reflective exoskeleton. Imago, 173.

200 Willow Longhorn, *Lamia textor*

Length, approx. 35 mm. Larvae of long-horned beetles can be recognized by the fact that they are broadest at the front. The larva of this longhorn lives on creeping willow – one of the few woody plants found on dunes – as well as on other willow species, on poplar and, in exceptional cases, on birch. The larva makes corridors in the xylem, especially in the lower part of the trunk and upper roots. Metamorphosis takes two years and towards its final stages a pupal chamber is made under the bark. Formation of the pupa (200a) takes place in this. Imago, 181.

HYMENOPTERA:
Ichneumons

201 *Banchus compressus*

Length, approx. 14 mm. This distinctive species of the Ichneumonidae can be seen on sand in early spring. Like the fly *Salmacia ornata* (315), parasitic on the larva of the noctuid *Agrotis vestigialis* (104) which feeds on the roots of marram and lyme grass and which is often found just under the surface of the sand, where it is an easy prey for parasites.

HYMENOPTERA: Solitary and Social Wasps

202 Ruby-tail, *Hedychrum nobile*

Length, 5–10 mm. Ruby-tail wasps are easily recognized by their vivid metallic colours, which are caused by diffraction of light in laminated structures of the exoskeleton. *H. nobile* is common in places where the digger wasp *Cerceris arenaria* (232) or other species of *Cerceris* breed in great numbers. The females fly low over the ground seeking out suitable nests. If a nest is fully stocked, an egg is deposited which soon hatches. The tiny larva locates the larva of the host insect and begins to suck its juices. The males are often seen in the flowers of devil's-bit.

203 Red Wasp, *Vespa* (=*Paravespula*) *rufa*

Length, 7–14 mm. Apparently the predominant social wasp in sandy areas. The nests are constructed underground, usually suspended from the roots of a tuft of grass or from a tree stump. This species is recognized by the somewhat red colour of the base of the abdomen, but the tint itself is frequently ill-defined.

204 Potter Wasp, *Eumenes pedunculatus*

Length, 10–17 mm. Rare. Similar to the British species, heath potter (*E. coarctata*). In its breeding habits this interesting insect shows complex patterns of behaviour. Its pitcher-shaped nest is made of clay collected from the banks of small ponds. With the mandibles the wasp rolls the clay into a ball, which is carried back to the selected nesting place, often at the foot of a tuft of grass, a stone, or a dead branch lying on the ground. A flat-bottomed bowl is formed with the help of the head and front legs. This bowl is gradually expanded and finally becomes a perfect pitcher-shape with a neat collar. The interior is constantly being smoothed out, whereas the outside is less even. When the nest is ready and the clay dry, an egg is deposited hanging from a thin thread on the inside of the pitcher near the opening. Then the hunt for prey begins. This consists of caterpillars of various geometrid moths, often *Ematurga atomaria* (93). Up to ten caterpillars are found in each pitcher. When the nest has been fully stocked, it is closed with a lump of clay.

205 *Pterocheilus phaleratus*

Length, 7–10 mm. Rare. The nests are made in the sand often on flat levels under the vegetation. A short corridor leads vertically down into the ground, where it widens into a cell, which is about 1 cm long and lies horizontally. The egg is suspended from the ceiling of the cell in the same way as the eggs of other solitary wasps, except that the thread is very short. Again the prey consists of caterpillars of geometrid moths.

206 Spiny Mason Wasp,
Odynerus spinipes

Length, 9–12 mm. Fairly common in Britain. The name refers to spines found only on the middle pair of thighs in the male. Breeds in steep walls where the material has a high clay content. A short corridor of 6–7 cm leads into two to five cells. Before provisioning starts, the wasp builds an entrance spout of clay, the opening of which is turned downwards. This is evidently a protection against such predators as ruby-tail wasps. An egg is suspended by a thin thread in each cell. The larvae feed on weevil larvae (*Phytonomus*), of which about 15 are placed in each cell. When the cell is fully stocked, it is closed with a lump of clay.

HYMENOPTERA: True Ants

207 *Formica rufibarbis*

Lengths, female 9–11 mm, worker 4–7.5 mm. A fairly common ant all over Denmark, mainly in open, sunny and warm localities with sparse vegetation. The nests are found underground and are usually difficult to find. The small entrance holes are often well hidden. There is only one female in each colony. The species hunts singly, does not follow 'ant roads' fixed by scent and is a fast-moving animal: it finds its bearings by sight and feeds mainly on other insects.

208 Negro Ant, *Formica fusca*

Lengths, female 7–10 mm, worker 3.5–6.5 mm. Found in dry as well as damp places and common and generally distributed. Its nests are established in widely different places; they are never made of plant material, but always of clay and sand; and colonies are usually small to medium. A fast-moving and timid ant, which feeds partly on honeydew and partly on insects. Flying castes arise in late summer.

209 Black Ant, *Lasius niger*

Lengths, female 8–9 mm, worker 3–5 mm. A particularly adaptable species which can be found almost everywhere, including dunes. It makes its nest in the ground, often under a stone or a piece of wooden planking. From the entrances the ants construct both open and covered tracks to plants infested by aphids. The food most sought after by the ants is honeydew from aphids and scale insects, but they also attack smaller insects and visit flowers to suck nectar. If their nests are damaged they attack their enemies vigorously. The nuptial flight takes place on calm, warm days in July–August.

HYMENOPTERA: Velvet 'Ants'

210 Black-headed Velvet-ant, *Myrmosa melanocephala*

Lengths, female 3–5 mm, male 7–11 mm. Shows a predilection in Britain for sandy situations. The females are very similar to red ants and are wingless. The males are considerably bigger, are very hairy and possess wings. They are parasites on various digger wasps, e.g. *Diodontus tristis* (223), *Lindenius albilabris* (234) and *Crabro* spp.

211 Ant-wasp, *Methoca ichneumonides*

Lengths, female 4–6 mm, male 10–14 mm. Widely distributed but local in Britain. Again the females (211a) are wingless and are very similar to red ants. The males have wings and closely resemble ichneumons. The larva of the brown tiger beetle (192) serves as a living larder for the larva of the ant wasp. When the female, mainly by means of her sense of smell, has located the burrow of the tiger beetle larva, she behaves in a manner which tends to lure this out, partly by running about around the opening, partly by waving her antennae in the burrow. If the tiger beetle larva emerges, the ant-wasp attacks it quickly with her sting. If the larva does not appear at the opening of the excavation, the ant-wasp crawls into the shaft, paralyses the larva

and deposits her egg. She then leaves, closes the shaft and seeks another larva.

212 Large Velvet-ant, *Mutilla europaea*

Length, 11–15 mm. Fairly common locally in Britain. A parasite on various bumble-bees living in the ground, on each larva of which the female lays an egg. It is said that a *Mutilla* attack can totally destroy a bumble-bee nest. The females are capable of inflicting painful stings on man.

213 *Tiphia femorata*

Length, 10–14 mm. An insect of local occurrence in the south and east of England. The females can have reduced wings. They are often found in dunes, the males on inflorescences of wild carrot, the females running among lyme and marram grass, waving their antennae. They stop suddenly and begin to dig when they smell larvae of the dune cockchafer (198). The larva is paralysed by stinging, after which the egg is laid. At first the young *Tiphia* larva lives on the surface of the cockchafer; later it eats its way inside.

HYMENOPTERA: Spider-hunting Wasps

214 Spotted Ceropales, *Ceropales maculata*

Length, 5–11 mm. This genus, of which there are two species in

Britain, neither common, is specialized as a parasite on other spider-hunting wasps. The female is usually noticed flying low over the ground in search of a spider-hunting wasp in the process of dragging its own prey to its nest. If, for some reason, it leaves the prey for a moment, the female *maculata* quickly deposits an egg in one of the lung-books of the spider. Occasionally the female makes a direct attack on the host and a struggle ensues, during which the attacker may succeed in laying her egg. This is deposited before the host lays its own egg; it hatches sooner and the larval parasite kills the host larva when this emerges. As *Ceropales* is parasitic on different species of spider wasp, the size of the adult varies considerably.

215 Leaden Spider Wasp,
Pompilus plumbeus

Length, 5–10 mm. Typical of yellow dunes, where the females are often seen preparing for the next generation. The burrows, about 5 cm deep, are made in loose, shifting sand. The males, often smaller and less hairy than the females, fly in search of un-paired mates. *Pompilus* preys on wolf spiders, notably *Arctosa perita* (335), the colour of which blends with the sand. After the spider has been paralysed, it is temporarily buried a few millimetres under the surface. (At this time it is particu-

larly liable to attack by the parasitic wasp *Ceropales maculata* which lays its egg in one of the spider's lung-books.) When the female has finished her burrow she fetches the spider and places it in the nest, after which this is closed and its entrance camouflaged. Among the black-and-red spider hunting wasps are several species, including the common *Pompilus spissus*, which is recognized by the absence of the comb-like spines on its fore-feet. Their breeding behaviour differs from that of other spider-hunting wasps in that they catch the wolf spider while this is in its underground retreat. By using her mandibles the wasp works her way through the material on top of the spider's lair. This consists mainly of pine-needles, small pieces of bark, lichen and similar plant litter. She then locates the prey, paralyses it and lays her egg. The species does not make a nest, but the entrance to the spider's retreat is closed and camouflaged after the egg has been deposited.

216 Dark Anoplius, *Anoplius fuscus*

Length, 10–14 mm. A common British species of wide distribution which can be seen throughout the summer in sandy localities. The fertilized females over-winter and in spring begin to dig their burrows and search for prey. They attack large wolf spiders, such as *Trochosa terricola* (*Field and Meadow*

Life, No. 503), which they paralyse by stinging them twice in the nerve centres of the cephalothorax. When, after a few seconds, the spider ceases to struggle, it is pulled to the nesting site. Here it is wedged temporarily between the shoots of a plant, while the nest is being finished. After the spider has been pulled into the completed burrow and the egg deposited, the entrance to the nest is closed and camouflaged.

HYMENOPTERA: Digger Wasps

217 *Astata stigma*
Length, 6–10 mm. A species of rather hot situations, which can be watched in the dry, lichen-covered areas behind the dunes, where the sun warms the sand. Among other preys it takes capsid bugs (*Lygaeidae*). The nest is built on level ground and consists of a single burrow with a cell at the base. The male is easily recognized by its large eyes, which meet on top of the head, and by the white spot on the forehead. Common in central and southern Europe.

218 *Miscophus ater*
Length, 4–5 mm. Found on south-facing sandy banks in June–July, where the females move rapidly in their search for small spiders. These they paralyse with two stings and carry to their nests. The excavation is a few centimetres deep and comprises a burrow ending in a single cell. The males are found in sunny places, often swarming around isolated bushes, from the leaves of which they take honeydew.

219 *Tachysphex ibericus borealis*
Length, 7–10 mm. Common everywhere in sandy areas, gravel pits and similar places. The nest, which is built in early June, consists of a single shaft, approximately 3 cm long, without branches. The prey is generally conveyed to the nest in flight and comprises paralysed grasshopper nymphs. Each nest is stocked with up to 12 of these. While the wasp is looking for prey, the entrance remains open.

220 *Tachysphex pompiliformis*
Length, 7–10 mm. Found in similar situations to those colonized by the previous species, but requires higher temperatures. A fast-moving animal, often difficult to follow with the eye because of the irregularity of its flight. It preys on the large nymphs of grasshoppers, which are often dragged overground to the nest. The egg is placed on the ventral side of the young grasshopper between the first and second pair of legs.

221 **Two-coloured Mimic Wasp,** *Psen equestris*
Length, 6–10 mm. A common British insect in summer on the

fringes of open heaths, where there are small stretches of bare sand between tufts of heather. It also breeds in steep banks along sandy paths. The nest, a very long burrow with branches, is often constructed below overhanging heather. The larvae feed on jumping plant lice (*Psyllidae*). Often the wasps live in colonies of 20 or more, with several species sharing the same locality.

222 Pale-footed Black Wasp,
Psenulus pallipes

Length, 5–9 mm. Structurally similar to *Psen* but the colour is always plain black. A protruding rhomboid area lies between the antennae. The species is often seen swarming around isolated fencing posts or pine stumps in sunny places, where the wasps clear the dust out of deserted insect burrows and use these for their nests. Like others of the genus, they prey on psyllids and aphids. The partitions between the individual cells are made from fine wood particles mixed with saliva.

223 Melancholy Black Wasp,
Diodontus tristis

Length, 5–8 mm. Often found in the same places as species of *Psen* (221), and often together with these, but also to be seen building its nest near roadsides where there is loose soil and sloping ground. Nests are often in colonies, each nest consisting of one main bur-

row, about 10 cm long, terminating in an enlarged cell. From the main shaft several side branches arise, and these again have branches. There are 10–15 cells in all, which are filled with aphids. *Myrmosa melanocephala* (210) is a parasite on the present species.

224 *Passaloecus roettgeni*

Length, 5–7 mm. Frequently to be seen swarming in the sunshine, often in numbers, around fencing posts. The nests are made in deserted insect burrows, which are cleaned out thoroughly. Preys on wingless aphids, of which 20–25 individuals are placed in each cell: the aphids are seized at the back of the head and their nerve centres destroyed by bites. Only in exceptional cases is the sting used. When a cell has been stocked, it is closed with a thin wall of resin: this, taken from pine trees, is also used to close the entrance hole after the entire nest has been provisioned. A closely related species, *P. turionum*, makes its nest in the deserted resin galls of the leaf roller, *Petrova* (*Evetria*) *resinella*.

225 *Nysson maculatus*

Length, 6–8 mm. Obtained only rarely in Britain. The species is fairly rare in Denmark but commoner in northern Germany (Lüneburg Heath, etc.). Occurs in sandy, sunny places at the edges of woods as well as in the area between grey dunes and pine woods.

The wasp does not build its own nest but is a parasite on another digger wasp, *Dienoplus tumidus*. When the female of this species has stocked her nest, this is closed. A female of *Nysson*, which has observed this process from a distance, now flies to the nest and digs into it. An egg is laid under the wings of one of the bugs taken as prey, where it is concealed from the owner of the nest, should she return. *Nysson* males are distinguished from the females by their first abdominal section, which is totally black.

226 Large Spurred Digger,
Nysson spinosus

Length, 8–12 mm. The commonest of the four species of *Nysson* in Britain. Its mode of life is generally similar to that of the previous species, the main difference being that the host is somewhat larger, being *Argogorytes mystaceus* (229) or perhaps *A. fargei*. It is a common phenomenon that closely related parasites prey on closely related hosts: in many cases the coloration of host and parasite are remarkably alike. Species of *Nysson* visit certain flowers, notably field scabious, devil's bit and sheep's bit.

227 Common Sand Wasp,
Ammophila sabulosa

Length, 15–25 mm. A particularly beautiful insect found throughout the summer in sandy areas near the British coast where the females,

restless and fussy in manner, are often seen digging nests or catching prey and the males gathering food on narrow-leaved hawkweed, sheep's bit or round-leaved campanula. Before catching and paralysing her prey – a caterpillar bigger than herself – the female excavates her nest, which consists of a vertical burrow expanded into a small cell at the bottom. The entrance is camouflaged with sand and gravel. The prey, paralysed by several stings in the thorax, is dragged to the nest which is often at a considerable distance. On the way, the wasp occasionally releases the larva in order to find the direction for her homeward journey. When the nest has been reopened the larva is pulled into it and a single egg deposited on the ventral surface. The nest is closed and camouflaged again and the wasp then seeks another breeding site. There is only a single egg in each shaft.

228 Great Sand Wasp,
Podalonia viatica

Length, 18–27 mm. Similar to the previous species, but somewhat stockier in build. The peduncle at the base of the abdomen is considerably shorter. The female searches out prey on the ground, running about with rapidly vibrating antennae. Suddenly she pauses in her search, begins to dig and can be seen pulling a large caterpillar (*Agrotis* or *Charaeas*) out of the ground. She paralyses this with several stings on the ventral side: finally the pharyngeal ganglia are crushed by bites. When the larva has been brought to the nesting place, it is temporarily inserted into a small bush or something similar. The mandibles are used for digging the nest. The nest burrow is only a few centimetres deep and widens at the base into a larva cell. The paralysed larva is brought down, an egg is deposited, the nest closed, the sand packed down and the site hidden with any available materials. Adult insects over-winter, and many are sometimes found together in old tree-stumps and the like.

229   Two-girdled Digger,
Argogorytes mystaceus

Length, 10–14 mm. Often seen building its nest in sunny situations and frequently near to *Hoplomerus reniformis*, *Mellinus arvensis* (231) or *Cerceris arenaria* (232). The main burrow of the nest usually penetrates vertically about 10 cm into the ground, then bends into a near-horizontal plane. Usually there are several larva cells in this section. It preys on the froghopper *Philaenus spumarius* (*Field and Meadow Life*, No. 83), the froth (cuckoo-spit) of which is ineffectual against this predator. *Nysson spinosus* (226) is found as a nest parasite in the present species and others of its genus. The males, easily recognized by their long antennae, perform pseudo-copulation with the flowers of certain wild orchids, by which these are pollinated.

230   Bee-killer Wasp,
Philanthus triangulum

Length, 12–14 mm. Rarely taken in Britain and mainly found in central and southern Europe, North Africa and Asia Minor. At a distance this species can look like the German wasp, but it is easily recognized by its triangular abdomen and its faster, more agile flight. It preys on honey-bee workers, which are attacked on various flowering plants. Although the bee is provided with her own defence, it is always the wasp which wins the battle, the motor centres of the bee quickly being put out of action by the sting of the wasp. The attacker often bites the head off the prey and sucks out the nectar-filled stomach before carrying the body to its nest. In regions where this wasp breeds in abundance it can cause a significant reduction in the honey-bee population.

231   Field Digger Wasp,
Mellinus arvensis

Length, 9–15 mm. A species fairly common in Britain from late July till early September. Preys on flies of the families *Calliphoridae*, *Tachinidae*, etc., which it finds on flowering plants or on fresh cow pats. The fly is attacked with a sudden leap from a distance of about 3 cm. It is held by the mandibles and the front legs, while the wasp bends its abdomen forwards and paralyses the prey with one or two stings. After a few seconds the fly stops moving and is flown to the nest. This is constructed in level as well as in sloping ground. Its main shaft has several side burrows each of which ends in a cell and each of which is eventually stocked with four to eight flies. The entrance to the nest is characteristic, some of the excavated material being built up around the hole like a small funnel.

232 Sand Tailed-digger,
Cerceris arenaria
Length, 13–16 mm. Common in sandy localities in the south of England and recognized by its size and the constrictions between the abdominal segments. The species is not particularly selective in its choice of breeding sites, but evidently prefers level sandy plains or small sandy slopes. Hundreds of females may build their nests in the same locality. The main burrow is approximately 10 cm deep, and from its bottom a number of short side branches come off, each ending in a cell. It preys on the bigger species of certain weevil genera, notably *Otiorrhynchus* and *Strophosomus*. Each cell is stocked with 10–15 individuals. The males are seen either swarming near the colony or

licking honeydew on oak leaves in sunny situations, sometimes in association with males of *Crabro cribrarius* (238), *Crossocerus wesmaeli* (236) and *Mellinus arvensis* (231). Common in June–July. The ruby-tail *Hedychrum nobile* (202) is parasitic on this species.

233 *Bembix rostrata*
Length, 16–20 mm. In Denmark, this strikingly beautiful and interesting insect used to be plentiful in the area around Tisvilde in North Zealand and on Bornholm, but these populations have disappeared, perhaps only temporarily. It remains fairly common on Öland and Gotland. The animals are often found in colonies of 10–30 individuals. The colonies are seen just behind the row of dunes farthest inland or on bare, sandy areas which are sheltered from the wind and exposed to the sun. A larval cell, stocked with such large dipterons as hover-flies (*Syrphidae*) or horse flies (*Tabanidae*), is constructed at the end of a burrow 15 cm long. Unlike other digger wasps, it does not stock the larval cell completely at one time. As soon as the first flies have been brought in, an egg is deposited and the nest closed. The larva soon hatches and begins to suck the body-juices of the prey. In the meantime the female catches more flies, which are carried into other shafts. At intervals these are opened and the larvae supplied

with additional food from them. The males are often seen swarming around the females while these are excavating.

234 *Lindenius albilabris*

Length, 5–8 mm. Usually builds in firm, sandy paths, often in groups of 10–20 individuals. The entrance to the nest is characteristic, because some of the sand which has been dug out comes to lie around the entrance hole, where it forms a crater. *Lindenius* preys on plantbugs, of which 10–22 individuals are found in each cell. While the female is searching for food, the entrance is left open. On returning she flies straight into the burrow without first alighting on the ground. The species is generally common where the soil is fairly loose and sandy. *Myrmosa melanocephala* (210) is a parasite on this wasp.

235 *Entomognathus brevis*

Length, 3·5–5·5 mm. A small, strongly built species, characterized by its rapid flight and sudden movements. Through a strong magnifying glass it can be seen that the compound eyes are thickly covered with hair. It breeds in sandy banks, gravel pits and similar places, often together with *Diodontus tristis* (223). It preys on small flea beetles (*Halticidae*), like *Longitarsus luridus*, *Chaetocnema concinna* and *C. hortensis* (*Field and Meadow Life*, No. 319). Both males

and females are often seen taking nectar from the flowers of field scabious, devil's bit and sheep's bit.

236 Wesmael's Digger,
      Crossocerus wesmaeli

Length, 3·5–6 mm. Very common everywhere in sandy soil, but most abundant on heaths and dunes, where the nests are built in the vertical faces of sandy slopes, often among the roots of lyme and marram grass in maritime situations. The larvae are fed on small flies and gnats, often of the families *Empididae* and *Chironomidae*. When the larva is fully developed, it spins a firm cocoon, the outside of which is covered with grains of sand. The adult males are often found in great numbers on oak leaves, where they sip honeydew.

237 Four-spotted Digger,
      Crossocerus quadrimaculatus

Length, 6–10 mm. Very common nearly everywhere in sandy areas, where it breeds in steep, sunny banks, often together with *C. wesmaeli* (236) and *Psen equestris* (221). At times it breeds in rotten wood. The nests are up to 20 cm long and the larval cells are furnished with stung flies and gnats of the families *Anthomyiidae* and *Culicidae*. When the larva is fully developed it spins a light brown parchment-like cocoon, the shape of which resembles an elongated pear.

238 Slender-bodied Digger,
Crabro cribrarius
Length, 12–17 mm. The males (238a) are characterized by the large, shovel-shaped expansions of their front tibia. The females are often seen swarming around or resting on sunny bushes and trees. The female catches prey – big flies like the gad-fly *Haematopota pluvialis* (267), assassin-flies (*Asilidae*), or bluebottles (*Calliphoridae*) – by hovering over leaves and then selecting a victim, swooping on it and paralysing it. Such a mode of attack fails fairly often. The nests, each of which usually has two or three cells, are built on the edge of sandy paths. The entrance is often hidden under a stone, a piece of wood or a similar object.

239 *Ectemnius continuus*
Length, 8–14 mm. This and the following species are characterized by the fact that they breed in dead wood – rotten fencing posts, dead pine trees or other old timber exposed to the sun. The nest, which is dug with the mandibles alone, consists of a short main shaft from the sides of which up to five burrows branch out, each ending in one or two cells. The larvae are provided with hover-flies (*Syrphidae*), bluebottles (*Calliphoridae*) and muscids (*Muscidae*), of which up to nine individuals are placed in

each cell. The males are seen in late summer, commonly on angelica.

240 Big-headed Digger,
Ectemnius cavifrons
Length, 8–16 mm. The nests are built in dead wood and the burrow system is often complex. Several side tunnels lead from a tortuous main burrow up to 35 cm long, and these often branch again. A reason for this is probably that several generations use the same entrance hole and continue to develop the existing burrow system. A single female probably provisions about eight cells in each complex. She preys on hover-flies like *Episyrphus balteatus* and *Syrphus ribesii* (*Field and Meadow Life*, No. 471), which she attacks on various flowering plants, often on umbellifers.

241 Common Spiny-digger,
Oxybelus uniglumis
Length, 3–7 mm. A species catholic in its choice of breeding sites which makes its nest between paving stones in yards as well as in sandy paths on dunes and heaths. The burrow is short and ends in a couple of cells, which are stocked with flies of the families *Anthomyiidae* and *Muscidae*. These are carried to the nest transfixed on the sting of the wasp, a method characteristic of species of *Oxybelus*. Common all over Britain. The ruby-tail *Hedychridium ardens* is a parasite on this wasp.

242 *Oxybelus lineatus*

Length, 6–9 mm. This exceptionally beautiful species is common in southern Europe. The nests are built in the same way as those of the previous wasp and the cells are provisioned with flies.

HYMENOPTERA: Solitary Bees

243 *Hylaeus confusa*

Length, 6–7 mm. About 17 species of the genus *Hylaeus* occur in the north and west of Europe. It is one of the most primitive of bee genera. As with cuckoo-bees there is no specialized apparatus on the body for gathering pollen. A bee collects its nectar and pollen in the stomach and, on returning to the nest, ejects the mixture as a viscous yellow paste. Nests are established in the hollow stems of raspberry, bramble, etc., or in holes in old timber. The bees are frequently seen in June and July on composite and umbelliferous inflorescences and can be found sheltering in campanulate flowers.

244 Girdled Colletes,
Colletes succinctus

Length, 9–11 mm. A species of wide distribution on heaths and commons in Britain. Species of *Colletes* build nests (often in colonies) in clayey or sandy banks. Burrows and cells of a nest are lined with secretions from the salivary glands, which form a silvery, transparent wall on setting. At the bases of their hind legs *Colletes* have long tufts of hair for holding pollen. The present species can be seen in June–September collecting pollen from the flowers of viper's bugloss, thyme and heather. The genus has a single generation every year and its larvae over-winter.

245 *Halictus tumulorum*

Lengths, female 7–8 mm, male slightly smaller. There are about 35 species of *Halictus* in north Europe. They accumulate pollen on their thighs. Several species can be seen from early spring to late autumn and consequently these have two generations in the year. After mating in August–September the males die, whereas the females over-winter buried in the sand or under moss. In spring the females appear again and begin to build their nests. The next generation appear in August and the fertilized females of this generation over-winter. The nests are built in sandy and clayey banks and paths, often in colonies. The genus *Halictus* is regarded as comprising social as well as solitary bees, since certain kinds, besides males and females, also have sterile workers like the bumble-bees and honey-bees. The present species is found mainly in sandy areas, where it can be seen on willow, cinquefoil, thyme and hawkweed.

246 *Epeolus variegatus*
Length, 6–8 mm. Only three species of *Epeolus* are known in Denmark. These are parasites, the females depositing their eggs in the nests of other bees. The *Epeolus* larvae hatch before the host larvae and consequently they are able to eat the food collected by the host bee. The host larvae either starve to death or are directly killed by the parasitic larvae. Like all parasitic bees the adults lack a pollen-collecting apparatus. Species of *Epeolus* are seen in mid- and late summer, flying low over the nesting sites of their hosts. *Colletes succinctus* (244) is one of the species parasitized.

247 **Silvery Leaf-cutter,**
Megachile argentata
Length, 8–11 mm. There are seven leaf-cutter species in Britain but the genus is widely distributed all over the world and there are thought to be at least a thousand species in all. The British leaf-cutters are small to medium insects, 8–15 mm long, but in the tropics there are species up to 35 mm long. Leaf-cutters gather pollen in a long brush on the ventral side of the abdomen, whereas most bees use the special hair on their hind legs. Species of *Andrena* and *Halictus* for instance, collect it on the thigh and species of *Bombus* on the tibia. This, the smallest British species, is known on most coastal dunes, where its nests are built in the dune sand or in sandy banks. Cells are lined with oval pieces of leaf, often from willow or with petals of bird's-foot trefoil, which the bee cuts with its mandibles. The species, seen frequently from the end of June till August, visits bird's-foot trefoil and clover.

248 **Leaf-cutter,** *Megachile circumcincta*
Length, 11–13 mm. The pollen-collecting apparatus of the female is red and black, whereas that of the small *M. argentata* (247) is completely white. Most leaf-cutters have a reddish pollen-brush. The males have enlarged forefeet used when gripping the females. Many build their nests in old timber, others excavate holes in the ground or in banks. *M. circumcincta* lives in the ground. The cells are lined with pieces of leaf from birch, etc. Often seen in June–August, when it visits bird's-foot trefoil, everlasting pea, clover and thistles.

249 **Mason Bee,** *Osmia maritima*
Length, 13–14 mm. This is the largest representative of the 14 species of mason bees found in Denmark. Like leaf-cutting bees, the masons collect pollen on their abdomens. They show a remarkable variety in their choice of breeding places and nest materials. They build their nests in bramble stems, key holes, shells and clay walls, or construct cells on stones and walls, or live in the ground.

The walls and partitions of the cells are made of clay, resin or chewed leaves and lichen. *O. maritima* is known in coastal areas with dunes. It digs its nest in the sand next to the roots of grasses, etc. This lies 4–6 cm down and contains one cell only, which is made of chewed vegetable matter mixed with stony grit. The bee is on the wing in June–July when it can be found on bird's-foot trefoil, restharrow and speedwell.

250 *Coelioxys elongatus*
Lengths, female 12–13 mm, male 11–12 mm. Leaf-cutters are parasitized by bees of the small genus *Coelioxys*. About six kinds are found in Britain. Being parasitic, they have no apparatus for the collection of pollen and are almost hairless. The females are easily recognized by their conical, pointed abdomen. The males have six processes on the last segment. The bees can frequently be seen in July–September flying to and fro in front of the nests of their hosts, but can also be found in the flowers of clover and the heads of composites. The present species is parasitic on various leaf-cutter species, including *Megachile argentata* (247) and *M. circumcincta* (248).

251 *Sphecodes pellucidus*
Length, 7–9 mm. There are about a dozen reputed British species of *Sphecodes*, all much alike and difficult to separate. All are parasites on the genera *Andrena* and *Halictus*, and are often seen flying low over sandy roads and paths where the host bees have their nests. As in the case of *Halictus* the larval stage is short and the fertilized females over-winter. In our climate there is only one generation in the year. This species can be found from May–September. In early summer it frequents willow and dandelion, in late summer, umbellifers.

252 **Nomad Bee,** *Nomada flavopicta*
Length, 9–10 mm. More than 20 representatives of *Nomada* are found in Britain and like others of the group are parasites on solitary bees. This particular form is a parasite on the genera *Andrena* and *Halictus* as well as on *Dasypoda hirtipes* (255). It can be seen in July–August on flowering thyme and heather and flying low over ground where the hosts are nesting.

253 **Nomad Bee,** *Nomada rufipes*
Length, 7–9 mm. A somewhat smaller nomad which is also parasitic on various members of the genera *Andrena* and *Halictus* as well as on *Colletes succinctus* (244). It can be seen in July–September flying low over ground where the hosts have their nests, or on the flowers of thyme, heather and broom.

254 *Panurgus banksianus*

Length, 10–11 mm. Only two species of *Panurgus* occur in Britain and both apparently prefer sandy areas. They often nest in colonies on sandy, dry paths or at roadsides with sparse vegetation. The bee is described as a thigh collector but it does, in fact, collect pollen over the whole of its body, as it lies in the flower so as virtually to bathe in pollen. Common in July–August on composites, where it can be seen resting in the flowers. In bad weather it can be found sheltering in bell-flowers.

255 **Hairy-legged Mining Bee,**
Dasypoda hirtipes

Length, 13–15 mm. Like members of the genus *Panurgus* it lives in colonies. Its nests are generally in sandy hills or disused gravel pits near the coast. The entrance hole is often framed by a small sand bank. The nest is an unlined excavation in sand. The main burrow can be up to 50 cm long and from this side burrows branch out, each ending in a cell. Very long hairs on the thighs and tibia are used for collection of pollen but, like the genus *Panurgus*, species of *Dasypoda* really gather pollen with the whole of the body, while performing virtual somersaults in the flowers. In Britain, *hirtipes* is fairly common in July–August, when it often visits inflorescences of composites like hawkweed, knapweed and chicory.

256 **Mining Bee,** *Andrena*
fuscipes

Length, 10–12 mm. The majority of the 60 British species of the genus *Andrena* are liable to be confused with honey bees. They make their nests in loose and sandy soil, such as lies on small paths or on dry, grass-covered banks, nearly always in colonies, which can have from four to several hundred burrows next to each other. The nest consists of one long main shaft with several side burrows, each ending in a cell, the sides of which seem to be polished as a result of secretions from the bee's salivary glands. Most of the species appear in early spring and can be seen on willow catkins, forsythia and other spring flowers. However, this species is not seen till August–September and then almost exclusively in heather districts.

257 **Mining Bee,** *Andrena*
hattorfiana

Length, 13–15 mm. One of the biggest species of *Andrena*. Like all *Andrenae* it collects pollen on the thighs, using the long yellow-white hairs on the hind legs. Fairly common in July–August in sandy areas, where it visits field scabious and sheep's bit.

258 **Mining Bee,** *Andrena vaga*

Length, 13–15 mm. In Denmark, known only on Zealand, where it appears very early in the year, the first insects being seen at the end of March and the beginning of April. These have disappeared already by mid-May. There are large colonies in sandy areas, often where there is sparse vegetation. The bee visits violet and the catkins of willow. A peculiar small beetle belonging to the *Strepsiptera* (323) is a parasite on the Danish colonies.

HYMENOPTERA: Social Bees

259 Bumble-bee, *Bombus variabilis*

Lengths, queen 16–18 mm, workers and males smaller. Rare. Unlike all other wild bees in Europe the bumbles are social, their society consisting not only of males and females but also of workers (sterile females) whose function is to take over from the queen the collection of food and the feeding of larvae. Young fertilized queens of this species bury themselves in the ground in the autumn, overwinter here and do not appear till June, when they seek a suitable place for nest-building. The nest itself is often placed in a tuft of grass on the surface of the ground. The first workers appear three or four weeks after the eggs have been laid. As the number of workers increases the queen spends less time feeding the larvae and eventually becomes merely an egg-layer. The new queens and males appear in August. After fertilization the queens bury themselves, whereas the males, workers and old queens

die off during autumn. Bumble-bees use the tibia of the hind legs as a basket for the collection of pollen. The coloration of this species can vary considerably from brown to orange.

260 Heath Bumble-bee, *Bombus jonellus*

Lengths, queen 15–20 mm, workers and males smaller. Widely distributed in the north and west of Britain but almost restricted to places where heather and bilberry are dominant. Unlike the previous bumble-bee, this one is about very early in the year. The queen, which has hibernated, appears in April. The first workers are seen at the end of May and the new queens and males in July. The heath bumble makes its nest in holes in the ground, such as empty mouse tunnels.

DIPTERA: Crane-flies

261 Daddy-long-legs, *Tipula juncea*

Length, 15–25 mm. Crane-flies (daddy-long-legs) are normally found in damp places with abundant vegetation, but this species is characteristic of dunes, moors and pine plantations. In central Europe it is seen on the wing from the middle of May till the middle of June, in northern Europe 2–3 weeks later. The female lays her eggs in open, damp, sandy surfaces. When she oviposits, she inserts her long abdomen far into the ground so that the wings and legs are spread out flat on the surface. The larvae feed on plant roots.

262 *Aspistes berolinensis*
Length, 2–3 mm. A small insect found in Danish coastal dunes from the end of June till the beginning of September. The adults are capable of digging long burrows in the sand and the larvae live here. The pupae are also able to bury themselves in sand if they happen to become exposed.

DIPTERA: Clegs

263 *Atylotus rusticus*
Length, 11–16 mm. Species of *Atylotus* can be distinguished from other large clegs by their pale colour and the fact that the mark on the front of the female's head is very small. The female sucks blood from human beings, horses, cattle and dogs. The present one is fairly common in warm places near the coast, where it is about in midsummer.

264 *Tabanus sudeticus*
Length, 20–27 mm. One of the largest of all British flies. Mostly confined to old forest areas, where it is probably associated with heather bogs. It can fly long distances and produces a deep and loud buzz on the wing. The larva is unknown, but probably lives in peaty soil, mud and *Sphagnum* moss.

265 *Hybomitra montana*
Length, 12·5–16 mm. Several species of *Hybomitra* are common. They can be distinguished from *Atylotus* and *Tabanus* by their hairy eyes. This one occurs on heath and dune areas where it often swarms around human beings on hot summer days, but seldom bites. The larvae live in mud and damp soil and are predatory, sucking the juices of other larvae and of worms.

266 **Thunder-fly,** *Chrysops relictus*
Length, 9–11 mm. One of the commonest members of the genus throughout Europe and seen in widely different habitats, including dunes and heaths. On the wing in June–August. The females feed actively on hot days and can cause painful bites, often attacking bathers on the beach. The larvae, found in water, are predatory.

267 **Gad-fly,** *Haematopota pluvialis*
Length, 8–13 mm. Found throughout Britain but commonest in the south. In close, sultry weather it can be a great nuisance because of its almost soundless approach during attack. The larva lives in damp soil.

DIPTERA: Snipe-flies

268 *Rhagio tringaria*
Length, 8·5–14 mm. Most species of *Rhagio* are found in woods, but

this one is also common in meadows, marshes and dune areas. It is a late insect which does not appear till July and can be seen till late September. Snipe-flies are predatory animals, which attack and suck the fluids of other insects. The larvae live in the ground and are also predatory, *R. tringaria* feeding upon small earthworms in leaf-mould or decaying timber.

DIPTERA: Bee Flies

269 *Phthiria pulicaria*
Length, 2·5–4 mm. The smallest of the British bee flies. It is a common insect in suitable localities, in and near coastal dunes, and can be discovered in most parts of the country. It flies from the middle of June till the end of July. It is said sometimes to occur in numbers in such composite inflorescences as mouse-ear, hawkweed and cat's-ear. Little is known of its biology.

270 Great Bee Fly, *Bombylius major*
Length, 7–12 mm. Generally distributed over the southern half of Britain where it flies early in the year, from mid-March until May. It can often be seen buzzing in front of flowers and with its long proboscis inserted in them. It shows a predilection for blue corollas. It can also be seen hovering over open areas exposed to the sun, where its hosts, various solitary bees of the genera *Andrena*,

Colletes and *Halictus*, are living in the ground. The eggs are deposited in sand and the tiny larvae, which are very mobile, find their own way into the nest burrows of the bees. Here they eat the bee larvae and the food collected for them.

271 *Systoechus sulphureus*
Length, 4–6·5 mm. Somewhat similar to the previous species, but smaller with wings of more uniform colour. Common in suitable habitats in Jutland, i.e. in coastal dunes and on inland moors. Also found in a few places on the Islands. On the wing from the middle of June to the beginning of August. The larvae are similar to those of 270, but are parasites on the egg pods of grasshoppers.

272 *Thyridanthrax fenestratus*
Length, 8–12 mm. A striking species, more or less confined to sandy heaths such as occur in Surrey, Hampshire and Dorset. Flies from the beginning of June till late September. The larva is parasitic on the egg pods of grasshoppers.

273 *Anthrax anthrax*
Length, 7–12 mm. One of the two north-west European species of a genus which comprises many forms in southern and eastern Europe. Rare. Similar to the following type but can be distinguished by the brush of small hairs on the ends of the antennae

(visible only under a magnifying glass). Little is known of its behaviour.

274 *Hemipenthes morio*
Length, 5–12 mm. As is the case of other parasitic insects its size varies considerably, depending on the amount of food available to the larva. The species is a hyper-parasite, feeding on the living larvae and pupae of ichneumons (201) and parasite flies (315–317) which attack butterfly larvae. In Jutland, only found north of Limfjorden, but can also be seen on Laesø in North Zealand, and on Lolland and Bornholm. In flight from the beginning of June to the middle of August.

275 *Exoprosopa capucina*
Length, 9–12 mm. Not British. Bee flies are widely distributed in warm and dry parts of the world; the fauna of northern Europe is in this respect poor in comparison with that of southern Europe. *Exoprosopa* is a genus with many southern European representatives, of which only the one illustrated here reaches Denmark, and even then only the southernmost part of Jutland. It has not been found in the Scandinavian peninsular. Little is known of its mode of life.

276 *Villa modesta*
Length, 10–13 mm. Species of *Villa* are parasites on the larvae and pupae of some of the larger moths (noctuids and silk moths).

The female collects fine grains of sand in a chamber on the tip of the abdomen. The grains surround the eggs as a protective shell when these are deposited, which is done during flight. The eggs are dropped around stones and solitary plants, and the tiny larva is very active and locates its own host. It works its way into the host's tissues and then changes its appearance so that it comes to look like a completely different insect. Only one larva develops in each host. Mainly a coastal insect which flies from the beginning of July to the middle of September.

DIPTERA: Robber Flies (Assassin Flies)

277 *Lasiopogon cinctus*
Length, 7·5–10 mm. This small un-distinguished-looking assassin fly is frequently found in Britain during early summer in dry and sandy places in woods as well as on such open land as dunes and beaches. It can be seen sitting on poles, stones and pathways, watching for prey – mainly gnats and flies. The female bores the tip of her abdomen down into loose, sandy soil when laying her eggs.

278 *Dasypogon diadema*
Length, 15–24 mm. This characteristic assassin fly is not British, but a common insect in sandy areas with scrub vegetation in central, western and southern Europe. Seen in July–August.

279 *Rhadiurgus variabilis*
Length, 11–14 mm. Uncommon. Seen in such sandy places as clearings in plantations and dunes, often at rest on the ground. Preys on the smaller kinds of moth, and on flies, capsid bugs, etc. The female deposits her eggs by walking around on the ground and attaching them one by one to twigs, pine needles, moss stems and similar objects. On hatching, the larvae work their way into the sand, where further development takes place.

280 *Asilus crabroniformis*
Length, 18–26 mm. This and 264 are among the biggest of British flies. Found generally throughout the country in clearings in plantations as well as in sandy fields and heaths and can often be seen sitting on the ground, but prefers to rest on cow and horse dung. The flight is heavy and noisy. It often moves several hundred metres when disturbed. Preys on grasshoppers and flies. The female deposits her eggs in masses of dung. The larva is up to 32 mm long.

281 *Dysmachus trigonus*
Length, 10–16 mm. Recognized by the short, high shape of the body and by the long hairs on the upper side of the thorax. Seen chiefly on beaches and dunes, but also found in sandy fields. On the wing in June and in the first half of July. Eggs are deposited in the spikes of various grasses, from where the newly hatched larvae fall to the ground.

282 *Machimus rusticus*
Length, 15–23 mm. Not found in Britain. Species of *Machimus* which occur in this country, are not typical of dunes and moors. The present species can be found infrequently in sandy places in southern and central Europe. Larvae of this and other robber flies are very like 321.

283 *Antipalus varipes*
Length, 16–19 mm. Found on open, sandy spots in coniferous forests, but otherwise little is known of its biology. In Denmark, has only been obtained near Frederikshavn in Jutland; and on the Islands more commonly in suitable habitats in North Zealand. Flies from June till the middle of August.

284 *Philonicus albiceps*
Length, 13–20 mm. Probably the commonest robber fly in British coastal and dune areas. The species is widely distributed and is found not only near coasts but occasionally in sandy places inland. On the wing in July and August. Usually it hunts its prey from the surface of the sand, where it can be seen sitting with its legs spread out and its abdomen resting on the ground. It tends to be easily

alarmed and moves a considerable distance when disturbed. It preys on various flies and lays eggs in loose sand, often on the leeward side of a dune among stems of marram and lyme grass. First the female removes the loose sand from a small area with the tip of the abdomen which forms a kind of spade with its long, upturned processes. Then the tip is pressed into the sand and the eggs deposited. Subsequently the site is again covered with sand.

DIPTERA: Stiletto Flies

285 *Thereva annulata*
Length, 8–11 mm. A common and widely distributed species, mainly found along the coasts, where it can occur in great numbers in suitable habitats, such as areas of shifting sand. Also found in sandy places inland. Flies from May till the middle of October. Males (illustrated here) have thick silver-grey hair. They make practice flights from the surface of the sand on warm days. The feeding habits of stiletto flies are uncertain. The larvae (320) live in the sand itself.

286 *Thereva marginula*
Length, 9–10 mm. Can be recognized by its short wings with brown spots and lines along the ribs. Seen in certain parts of southern Sweden as well as in central and southern Europe. Frequents warm, dry areas and flies in May–July.

DIPTERA: Soldier Flies

287 *Nemotelus uliginosus*
Length, 5–6·5 mm. *Nemotelus* species may be recognized by the forward prolongation of the lower part of the head, which gives the impression of a 'snout'. These small flies can often be netted in umbelliferous and composite flower-heads of plants growing in damp dune areas near pools of brackish water. The larvae live in water and tolerate a fairly high salt content. Species of *Nemotelus* are widespread but only near coasts. Seen from June till the middle of August. The males (287a) have a paler abdomen than the females (287).

288 *Stratiomys longicornis*
Length, 12–14 mm. One of the four British representatives of the genus. An early species (May–June) whose larvae, like those of the previous one, can survive in brackish water. Found mainly in coastal districts. The adult fly is usually to be seen on the umbels of such waterside vegetation as hemlock.

DIPTERA: Hover Flies (Syrphids)

289 *Pipizella varipes*
Length, 5–7 mm. This small, completely black species is to be seen from May to the beginning of September flying low over the ground with its abdomen lowered,

or basking on leaves and flowers. The larvae are found on the roots of umbellifers like parsley and parsnip, where they are useful in devouring aphids.

290 *Chilosia mutabilis*
Length, 6–8 mm. One of a large genus. A slender hover fly with a completely black body and a white middle section on its first pair of feet. Unlike the female, the male has hair on the eyes. Seen from the middle of June till the middle of August on many different flowers, including hawkbit and pimpernel, but seldom far from the coast. The larvae mine in plant tissues and are found in great numbers in the upper part of the tap-root of certain thistles. No doubt they also occur in other plants.

291 *Eumerus sabulonum*
Length, 5–8 mm. This species can be distinguished from others of the genus by the coloration on the second and fourth abdominal segments. It occurs singly in dry, sandy places, where it can be seen at rest on the ground or on plants. The larvae of some *Eumerus* species develop in cultivated bulbs and, in consequence, can become serious pests. Thus, the 'lesser bulb flies' *E. tuberculatus* and *E. strigatus* have been economic nuisances in the fenland districts of East Anglia. The food plant of the present species is unknown.

292 *Paragus tibialis*
Length, 4–6 mm. In northern Europe the insect usually has a near-black abdomen, but in the south individuals can be found with an extensive red coloration. Both the male and female have 'protruding' faces, which are yellow with a black stripe down the middle and a black shield without a yellow colour. This species is found particularly on dunes, where it flies low over the ground or rests on such plants as tormentil, biting stonecrop, sheep's bit and burnet rose. The larvae feed on aphids at the roots of sowthistle and knapweed.

293 *Chrysotoxum festivum*
Length, 11–15 mm. Darker-looking than most of the British species of *Chrysotoxum*, which are wasp-like flies with brilliant yellow abdominal arcs. In *festivum* the pale arcs do not extend over the sides of the abdomen. This species has four pairs of arcs, a dark line along the edge of the abdomen, long antennae and yellow legs. It is mainly seen on composite flowerheads like those of hawkbit and golden-rod.

294 *Chrysotoxum bicinctum*
Length, 10–13 mm. Differs from the other British representatives of *Chrysotoxum* in having only two clear yellow bows, a wide one on the second abdominal segment and a narrow one on the fourth. The coloration of these continues

along the sides. Usually found singly on leaves or flower-heads of umbellifers. It is thought that, like those of others of the genus, the larvae live on such dead organic matter as rotting wood.

295 *Didea intermedia*
Length, 9–13 mm. The three Danish representatives of *Didea* are very beautiful flies with black-and-yellow or greenish coloration and a characteristic curve in one of the transverse veins of the wings. The upper side of the abdomen is nearly flat. The species has a clear black middle stripe in the black face and fairly wide yellow cross-bands on the abdomen. It is only known in a few places in Denmark, but in Tisvilde Hegn and in northern Thy it has been netted in great numbers, especially in June, on the flowers of burnet rose, tormentil, common cat's ear, mouse-ear hawkweed, scentless chamomile and sheep's bit. Like the larvae of many other hover-flies with similar patterning, those of the present species are useful as destroyers of greenflies. It has been noticed that the insect sometimes lays eggs on aphid-infested gorse bushes.

296 *Sericomyia silentis*
Length, 14–18 mm. Similar to the two elegant, wasp-like flies, *S. borealis* and *S. lappona*, which are frequently encountered on wild, boggy moors such as occur on Dartmoor and in the New Forest.

Like these, *S. silentis* can be found in woods as well as in open country from the beginning of June till the middle of September. The larvae, which are of the rat-tailed type (see 298), develop in the water of bogs, where the oxygen tension may be low. Adults are often seen sitting on the ground or on leaves, but can also be discovered in various flowers like thyme and rose.

297 *Volucella bombylans*
Length, 11–16 mm. There are several colour variations of this very hairy hover-fly. The one illustrated here (*bombylans*) is black with a red abdominal tip and mimics the red-tailed bumble-bee, whereas *V. plumata* mimics buff-tailed bumble-bees. It has feathery antennae. The larvae (322) are found in the nests of garden bumble-bee, carder bee and red-tailed bumble-bee, as well as in those of some of the social wasps (*Vespa vulgaris* and *V. germanica*). They are useful as scavengers and devour dead pupae and other organic waste in the nests, the owners of which apparently tolerate their presence.

298 Drone-fly, *Eristalis intricaria*
Length, 11–14 mm. Several of the syrphids qualify for the designation 'drone-fly' on account of their resemblance to the male of the honey bee. The *Eristalis* illustrated here is one of the largest and most

112

hairy. The antennae are feathery. Its colour can vary considerably, some specimens having only black hairs on the thorax. In April it can be seen on willow catkins. It is common during the whole summer on many flowers and in autumn is found on heather. The larvae, so-called rat-tailed maggots, live in polluted water, where they get much of their oxygen through a telescopic breathing tube at the tail end which pierces the surface.

DIPTERA: Thick-headed Flies (Conopids)

299 Wasp-fly, *Sicus ferrugineus*
Length, 8–13 mm. Not uncommon in Britain on the outskirts of woods. All conopid flies are parasites when larvae and develop inside other insects, chiefly wasps and bees. The eggs are deposited directly in the abdomen of the host during flight. Usually there is a single egg in each host. It is estimated that up to 30% of all bumble-bees may be infested by wasp flies. It appears in June–August when it is seen on umbels, composites and bramble flowers.

DIPTERA: Empid Flies

300 *Platypalpus strigifrons*
Length, 2·5–3 mm. A representative of a large genus of very small flies. All the *Empididae* are predatory. Species of *Platypalpus* attack small insects like other flies and aphids, holding them in their legs, which close like a trap, while they suck the prey with their pointed proboscis. A typical dune insect which can be seen during the whole summer.

301 *Hilara lundbecki*
Length, 2·7–3·5 mm. There are more than 60 British species of *Hilara*. Males of the genus can be recognized by the dilation of the metatarsi of the first pair of legs. This part holds a spinning gland, the secretion of which is used for wrapping the prey, which is proffered to the female before mating, an act which occurs in flight. The males often swarm low over water. The present species is typical of localities near the coast and is common on moors where there are damp places. It is on the wing from the beginning of June till late August.

DIPTERA: Long-headed Flies

302 *Sciopus loewi*
Length, 5–6 mm. Like the empids (300–301) the long-headed flies (*Dolichopodidae*) are a large family. Most of them are found in damp places with rich vegetation. They are predatory and suck the body fluids of small, soft-skinned invertebrates. Species of *Sciopus* are some of the few long-headed flies found in dunes and on moors. Little is known of the natural history of the larvae.

DIPTERA: Shore Flies, Frit Flies, etc.

303 *Striphosoma sabulosum*
Length, under 2 mm. Belongs to the family *Anthomyzidae*. An aberrant species in which the wings are partly atrophied. Several small flies of various families found in the dunes cannot fly and have wings which are more or less reduced. The present one runs over the sand and jumps considerable distances when disturbed. About from late May to late July. The larvae develop under the leaf sheaths of grasses and sedges.

304 *Helcomyza ustulata* (= *Actora aestuum*)
Length, 6–10 mm. One of the familiar flies of the British seashore, where it gathers about the carcases of animals washed ashore. Several bigger flies are also found on the beach, representatives of *Coelopa*, *Fucellia* and *Scatophaga*, for example. People walking along the shore often find swarms of flies around their feet. *H. ustulata* can be distinguished from members of the other genera, since it moves at least 5–10 metres down wind when disturbed, whereas the other insects fly only short distances. The larva develops in rotting seaweed and the adult is on the wing in June–August.

305 *Tetanops myopina*
Length, 5–6 mm. A member of the family *Otitidae*. Inhabits sandy beaches and dunes. Common and widely distributed both on exposed and sheltered coasts. On the wing from the middle of June till late August. The larva is unknown.

306 *Trixoscelis obscurella*
Length, about 2 mm. A genus of very small flies. Two of the British species seem to be associated with coastal localities. *T. obscurella* is found on the higher part of the beach and in the first of the yellow dunes, often where sea purslane grows. The pupa can be found in the sand under this plant. The larva is unknown. The imago is on the wing from late June till the beginning of August and is most abundant in July.

307 *Chamaemyia*
(= *Ochthiphila*) *flavipalpis*
Length, 4–5 mm. Particularly common and widely distributed in seashore locations in Britain, on the dunes and on nearby heaths. The biology is interesting in that the larvae are predatory and suck aphids and coccids living on marram grass and lyme grass. Adults are on the wing in May–August.

308 *Minetta desmometopa*
Length, 4–5 mm. Representative of the family *Lauxaniidae* which, in Britain, comprises 13 genera and nearly 50 species. All are small flies of retiring habit. The larvae of *desmometopa* develop in rotting leaves. Found in association with sea buckthorn growing on dunes.

309 Frit-fly, *Meromyza pratorum*

Length, 5–6 mm. Several kinds of frit-flies (*Chloropidae*) inhabit moors and dune areas. The larvae colonize living plant tissues, especially the interiors of grass stems. Most are smaller than the species illustrated here and are black or black and yellow.

DIPTERA: Big-headed Flies

310 *Alloneura littoralis*

Length, 3–4 mm. The big-headed flies (*Pipunculidae*) have a particularly interesting mode of life, as the larvae are endoparasites within various bugs, locusts and grasshoppers. In some parts of the world certain big-headed flies are important biological controls against these pests. Only one larva develops in each victim, normally in the abdomen. The adults are not seen in flowers, but usually fly singly among vegetation. The female searches out a host insect and on locating one, quickly inserts her pointed ovipositor and deposits an egg. The host of the present species is unknown.

DIPTERA: Blow-flies, Flesh Flies, etc.

311 Green-bottle, *Lucilia sericata*

Length, 5–10 mm. Species of *Lucilia* are common everywhere. The adult flies are about throughout the summer on flowers, leaves and tree trunks. This species normally lays its eggs on dead animals and in rarer cases on dung. It is also attracted by open wounds and lays its eggs in these. The larvae then live on the dead tissue and pus. Formerly they were used to clear away suppurating tissue and promote the growth of healthy flesh. In Scotland, however, a species of *Lucilia* attacks the living tissues of sheep and causes considerable damage, often leading to the death of the host. Individuals vary considerably in size, depending on the quantity and quality of the food available to the larvae.

312 *Melinda agilis*

Length, 5–10 mm. Like the previous species the size varies considerably. Common on certain moors and dunes. Its larvae are said to develop as internal parasites of snails.

313 *Miltogramma punctatum*

Length, 6–10 mm. One of two British representatives of *Miltogramma*. This and the following species are members of the family *Sarcophaginae* and are features of warm, dry localities. They are parasites on digger wasps and mining bees. All are strong fliers which 'shadow' the host during its flight. At an opportune moment the fly either places an egg on the prey which the digger wasp is dragging home as food for its larva, or enters the bee's nest-burrow and deposits an egg on the honey and pollen mixture. The fly larvae develop faster than the wasp and bee larvae, which sooner or later starve to death. Not rare in suitable habitats in this country and appears in May–August.

314 *Metopia leucocephala*
Length, 4·5–7·5 mm. Closely allied to *Miltogramma*, with very similar habits, but rather more striking in appearance. There are two species of *Metopia* on the British list. Common near the coast, but also seen inland. The male with its silver-white forepart of the head is easily recognized. About from May to early August.

DIPTERA: Parasite Flies

315 *Salmacia* (=*Gonia*) *ornata*
Length, 8·5–11·5 mm. Appears early in the year (late March–June) and found in warm, dry places. The female deposits about 4000 eggs on grass leaves. The tiny larva enters its host with the food. The host is a moth larva, usually that of a noctuid like *Agrotis vestigialis* (104). Pupation takes place inside the host pupa.

316 *Larvaevora* (=*Echinomyia*) *fera*
Length, 9–14 mm. Another common parasite fly found in warm, dry places, but appearing in June–September. Often seen basking in the sun on sand. Its victims are various noctuid larvae, e.g. pine moth, broom moth and nun moth. The fly deposits eggs near the host or on the host's food plant. The tiny fly larva sits with its ventral side attached to the underlying surface. Periodically it raises the thorax and moves it back and forward. Should it touch a host larva, it attaches itself to this and works its way inside.

317 *Larvaevora* (=*Echinomyia*) *grossa*
Length, 15–20 mm. The largest British larvaevorid, closely related to the previous species, but bigger, completely black, more bristly and with a completely yellow head. Not rare and mainly seen on umbellifers and composites. Preys on various moth larvae, a common host being the caterpillar of the oak eggar (126). On the wing from June to mid-August.

DIPTERA: Muscid Flies

318 *Phorbia penicillaris*
Length, 5–7 mm. A representative of the family *Anthomyiinae* and characteristic of dunes. Several flies of the genus *Delia*, belonging to the same family, can be found in similar localities. All muscid larvae develop in plant material: those of the genus *Phorbia* probably live in the stems of marram and lyme grass. The ovipositor, shaped like a sickle, is used to make a cut in the plant tissue. Seen in May–June.

319 *Helina protuberans*
Length, 5·5–7 mm. Species of *Helina* are characterized by the pairs of dark spots on the abdomen. The present one can be found near the coasts and has the whitish-grey colour which is a feature of many dune animals. Processes on the tip of the female's abdomen are used for excavation. She buries her eggs in the sand. Appears early in the year, generally in May–June.

DIPTERA: Fly Larvae

320 Stiletto Fly, *Thereva* sp.
Length, up to 30 mm. The larvae of species of *Thereva* live in soil and sand. That of *T. annulata* (285) inhabits dunes where it moves just under the surface and makes a characteristic winding trail. A particularly active larva: if removed and laid on the surface it quickly bores its way into the sand again and if held in the hand it jumps like a twisted rubber band suddenly uncoiling. Predatory, sucking the body juices of insect larvae and pupae which it meets on its way through the sand. It can withstand partial starvation and desiccation for a considerable time. Over-winters and pupates in April–May.

321 Assassin Fly, *Machimus* sp.
Length, up to 24 mm. Larvae of several assassin flies are found in sandy soil. Various kinds can be distinguished from each other by the structure of their mouth parts. The larvae are found mainly among the root systems of herbs and bushes. It is uncertain whether they are predatory, herbivorous, or, what is most likely, omnivorous. Imago, 282.

322 Hover Fly, *Volucella* sp.
Length, up to 25 mm. Feeding habits of larvae of syrphid flies are varied. Larvae of some forms crawl over the foliage plants sucking aphids; others live inside plant tissues, such as stems and bulbs. *Volucella* larvae develop as scavengers in the nests of bumble-bees and social wasps. Imago, 297.

COLEOPTERA: Strepsiptera

323 *Stylops muelleri*
Lengths, male about 4 mm, female about 8 mm. Eleven species of *Stylops* are known in the British Isles. They represent a very peculiar group, in which the larvae are parasites on other insects, mainly wasps and bees. The species illustrated is parasitic on the mining-bee *Andrena vaga* (258). Only the winged male ever leaves the host. He has a single pair of large fan-like wings, with the elytra expanded into club-shaped organs. On the other hand, the female (323a) remains permanently in the bee's abdomen. Her head and thorax form a flat brown plate which protrudes between the host's abdominal seg-

ments (323b), whereas her abdomen is a soft sac lying inside the abdomen of the bee. *Andrena vaga* appears early in the year and on warm, sunny days *Stylops* males can occasionally be seen swarming around the nest holes of *Andrena* in search of the females inside the bees. A female *Stylops* produces numerous eggs from which develop thousands of tiny, active larvae, each only about ⅓ mm long. These leave the bee when she is visiting flowers, and later enter other bees, which transport them to their nests. They work their way into the bee larvae and here further development takes place. Stylopised bees have been found in *Andrena* colonies in widely scattered regions of Britain.

CHELONETHIDA: False Scorpions

324 *Neobisium muscorum*
Length, about 3 mm. Perhaps the commonest false scorpion in Europe. Found in dunes, as well as other ecosystems, where it occurs in sand under moss and lichen; and particularly in grey dunes with willow and crowberry. Feeds on springtails, and other small invertebrates, which it seizes with its chelae. The prey is broken up and at the same time, digestive juices are poured over it. Finally the liquid is sucked up. The species illustrated here undergoes indirect insemination. The male drops his spermatophores in the course of his wanderings. These have a stalk attached to the underlying surface. At the end of this stalk there is a small dilation containing a drop of seminal fluid. When the female finds a spermatophore she places herself over it and absorbs the drop in her genital opening. The eggs are carried by the female in a brood pouch.

ARANEAE: Spiders

325 *Eresus niger*
Lengths, female 10–15 mm, male 7–10 mm. None taken in Britain for nearly 70 years. Formerly known from parts of Dorset. An unmistakable species. Seen in open situations such as heathery coastal slopes. A tube approximately 10 cm long and 1 cm across is made in sandy soil. This shaft is lined with webbing which, on the surface of the soil, expands into a funnel. One side of the web is pulled over the opening and secured to various plants with long strands. A number of sticky threads, attached to these, form a snare. Even big beetles are sometimes caught. When the spider senses that prey has become enmeshed, it dashes forward, kills the animal and then drags it into the tube and sucks its juices. The female deposits her eggs in a white, lenticular egg cocoon, which is suspended in the top part of the nest. Approximately 80 young hatch from the egg cocoon and remain in the mother's lair until the following spring.

The female dies during the autumn. A species which does not become sexually mature for four years.

326 *Dictyna arundinacea*
Length, approximately 3·5 mm. A very common and widespread little spider in parts of Britain where there is uncultivated soil with low vegetation (e.g. moors). It spins its web in the top of grass or heather bushes. This consists of a number of long strands spreading out from the top with sticky threads attached in a criss-cross pattern. Relatively large insects may be caught in this snare. Mating is in June in a nuptial chamber which the male spins inside the female's web system. During the summer the female makes up to half a dozen egg cocoons in the central part of the web, with about 18 eggs in each.

327 *Philodromus fallax*
Length, about 5 mm. Confined to sandy places, notably coastal sand dunes, where it is widespread in Britain, although not always easy to discover because of its imitative colouring. Snare, 345.

328 *Xysticus cristatus*
Length, 4–7 mm. The most widespread species of the genus in Britain. Like the previous species a crab spider (*Thomisidae*), the name referring to the fact that both the form and movement suggest those of a crab. Prey is taken while the spider sits quite still either on the ground or in the vegetation waiting for it. Should the prey touch the forefeet, the spider immediately seizes it. This species lives in such low vegetation as heather. The pattern of mating is peculiar. The male grabs one of the female's forelegs and crawls on to her back. If she remains still, the male spins a web attaching the female's cephalothorax and feet to the ground. When the female has been secured in this way mating takes place, the male several times inserting his pedipalps into her epigyne. Afterwards the female escapes from the web with difficulty. The cocoon is placed under stones or in vegetation and the female guards it until the young hatch.

329 *Clubiona similis*
Length, about 7 mm. About 18 *Clubiona* species occur in Britain. All are found in vegetation and are nocturnal animals which, after sundown, move slowly over twigs and leaves in search of prey. During the day they hide in their retreat, shaped like an oblong bag and spun between leaves. The species illustrated occurs near the sea in marram and lyme grass vegetation.

330 *Tibellus maritimus*
Length, 8–10 mm. Widespread in sandhills and rough ground in

Britain. One of several species of spider which have become adapted in shape for resting on a narrow grass leaf. The body is elongated with two pairs of legs forwardly directed and two pairs pointing backwards. One of the crab spiders, catching its prey in the vegetation after the manner of 328. The flat egg cocoon is of irregular shape. It is placed in vegetation and the female usually guards it.

331 *Agroeca proxima*
Length, 6–8 mm. This spider – one of the tube spinners (*Clubionidae*) – is not seen very often, being nocturnal in habit, although widespread in Britain and common locally. It does not spin a snare, but chases its prey or surprises sleeping insects. Occurs in tufts of marram grass near coasts as well as in moss on moors and in woods. The egg cocoon is carrot-shaped and suspended by a stalk, as shown and described for 344.

332 *Aelurillus v-insignitus*
Length, female 6–7 mm, male 4–5 mm. Uncommon, occurring in Britain only in the southern counties among low undergrowths on heaths. This and the following species are both jumping spiders (*Salticidae*). These can be recognized by the cephalothorax, which is flat on top and broadest near the front. There are three rows of eyes. The two centre eyes of the first row are particularly

large and structured so that the retina can be shifted relative to the lens. This means that the jumping spider receives a sharp, dimensional image of its prey. The legs are all of the same length, but the first pair are stronger than the others. A jumping spider is typically diurnal and most active in sunshine. It catches its prey by leaping upon it from a distance. This species is found in yellow dunes, where it is difficult to see against the sand. In cool, overcast weather it makes a hole in the sand, lies on its back in this, and covers itself with threads, which are camouflaged with sand grains.

333 *Hyctia nivoyi*
Length, 4–6 mm. A rare jumping spider, occurring on sandhills and in marshy areas south of Yorkshire. Like 330 has become adapted for living in tufts of marram grass, on the foliage of which it is difficult to see. The forelegs are well developed. Jumping spiders have a peculiar mating behaviour. The male alternately lifts first one and then the other of his first pair of legs in front of the female, at the same time raising his cephalothorax with the help of his second pair of legs. In this way he displays strong coloration on the forelegs and the light colour on the ventral side. If the female remains still, the male approaches her and repeats his display. Finally, mating takes place.

334 *Lycosa monticola*

Length, 5–6 mm. Widespread and rather common, locally abundant on heaths and commons through-out Britain. Everybody knows the fast-moving wolf-spiders, which can be found in incredible num-bers in almost any locality from very early spring. They do not spin a snare, but leap on their prey – hence the name *Lycosa* (=wolf). These spiders move exclusively overground and always spin a safety thread, although this seems to be superfluous. The eggs are carried in a cocoon fastened to the spinnerets on the tip of the ab-domen. The young remain cling-ing to the mother for the first couple of days. Most *Lycosa* species occur in damp situations, but the species illustrated here is mainly found in drier places.

335 *Arctosa perita*

Length, 6·5–8 mm. Frequent on dry heaths and in sandy localities in Britain where, although it forms a burrow, it is often seen running about in the sunshine. This wolf-spider lives in a Y-shaped tube, up to 20 cm deep and lined with thin silk. One of the limbs of the tube is open to the surroundings, and the spider sits here watching for prey. If a beetle or fly approaches, the spider leaps out and catches the insect. The female isolates herself in the tube when she is guarding her eggs. In July the female can be seen on the sand with her young on her back. In autumn both older and younger individuals bury them-selves in dry sand. A related spe-cies, *Trochosa cinerea*, is found on the beach where the sand is damper.

336 *Tarentula fabrilis*

Length, 10–16 mm. In Britain, this large, dark wolf-spider is known only at Bloxworth Heath, Dorset. Like the previous species, it spends most of its time in a short, vertical tube in the sand. A wall of sand grains is placed around the opening of the tube and is secured with a web. The spider sits in the opening and catches such passing insects as the nymphs of grasshoppers. Two broods may be hatched in a year, the first in June, the second in August. The female sits hidden in her egg cocoon until the young emerge. For the first two days they remain on her back.

337 *Pisaura mirabilis*

Length, 12–15 mm. Common almost everywhere in long grass, heather and open woods. Belongs to the family *Pisauridae* which is closely related to wolf-spiders (334–336), but which can be distinguished from these by the fact that its members carry their egg cocoon in the jaws and not attached to the spinnerets. The species has neither snare nor re-treat in which to live. It crawls about in the vegetation surprising its prey, which consists of flies, beetles and butterflies. During the mating season (May–June) the male places a drop of sperm on a small web which has been spun previously. The sperm is then drawn up into his pedipalps which are used for insemination. He catches a fly, spins a web of many layers around it, and carries it between his jaws to the female. The female accepts the fly and sucks it during mating, which can last up to one hour. The big, spherical egg cocoon is carried around in the jaws. Later a big nursery tent is made in which the young live for some time. Usually breeds twice during the summer.

338 Labyrinth Spider,
Agelena labyrinthica

Length, 8–12 mm. Common and locally abundant in the southern counties of Britain. Very similar to the house-spider, but has more distinct markings on the abdomen and is only found out of doors, especially in heather and dry grass. It spins a large web, which consists of a vertical retreat-tube which, at the top, widens into a closely woven carpet of consider-able size. Over this carpet threads are stretched in a criss-cross pattern up to a height of 30 cm. Flying and jumping insects which hit these threads fall down into the web, whereupon the spider

leaps out and kills them. Mating takes place in late summer on the female's carpet. The female re-mains completely passive during mating, pulling her legs close to the cephalothorax and lying as if she were dead. The egg cocoon, containing approximately 60 eggs, is suspended in a bag-shaped retreat, which has been spun near the snare. The young hatch during October but remain in the egg cocoon until the following spring.

339 *Araneus adiantus*
Length, 6–8 mm. Uncommon, and not recorded north of Cambridge-shire and Norfolk. This and the following species are orb-spinners (*Argiopidae*), to which the well-known cross spider also belongs. *A. adiantus* remains close to the ground and usually suspends its web on heather. The web is not large and has a small, close-woven centre and a bell-shaped nest spun over it.

340 *Araneus redii*
Length, 3·5–7 mm. Local, but then considerable numbers may be found close together, usually on heather, gorse, etc. Distributed all over the British Isles, but most frequent in the south. Its presence is betrayed by the characteristic moss-green egg cocoon (347) suspended from the top of heather or grass. These cocoons are mainly seen in June and each contains 66–132 eggs. They are not guarded by the female, which is thought to

die after ovipositing. The spider lives on a small, close-woven carpet close to the snare.

341 *Lithyphantes albomaculatus*
Length, 5–6 mm. This small spider is a rare species of southern counties in Britain, where it inhabits sandy fields with sparse vegetation and stones. Its snare is stretched between stones and plants, and consists of a carpet-like web suspended only about 2 cm above the surface of the ground by a few threads stretching from higher points. From the carpet a number of threads extend downwards to the surface of the sand. These are sticky at the bottom. If an ant, for example, touches one of them it sticks to it and its movements loosen the thread. As the thread is elastic it contracts, lifting the ant from the sand so that it becomes easy prey for the spider. A darker colour variation (341a) is also found. This and the following two species belong to the family *Theridiidae*, recognizable by the shape of the abdomen.

342 *Theridion sisyphium*
Length, 3–4 mm. A common spider all over the British Isles on heaths and dry situations elsewhere. The snare is fixed in bushes of heather, gorse, bramble, juniper, etc. It is an irregular, three-dimensional structure used for catching insects on the wing. There is a hood-shaped retreat

in the middle, and in this the spider has its egg cocoon. The young appear in July and, in their early stages, are given food regurgitated by the mother.

343 *Theridion saxatile*
Length, about 3·5 mm. Rather rare in Britain, but recorded from southern counties. It spins its snare near the ground, often on a small slope along a sandy road, or under stones at the base of a wall. From this, vertical threads stretch downwards. The bottom half centimetre of these are sticky (note also 341). The prey consists mainly of ants, which become stuck to the threads. When this happens the spider uses its forelegs to draw up its victims in much the same way as a bucket is pulled up from a well. These captives are removed to the retreat in the snare – see 346.

ARANEAE: Spiders' Webs
344 *Agroeca brunnea*
This small, white, bell-shaped egg cocoon is often seen in the tops of heather bushes. The web is attached by a vertical stalk and the inside divided into two compartments: the upper an egg chamber, the lower a bigger chamber, open at the bottom, in which the young live. The web is often covered with soil particles (344a). It is thought, but not established for certain, that the bell is made by *Agroeca brunnea* (a

close relative of 331) which, in Britain, is widespread but not common and is mainly a woodland spider.

345 *Philodromus fallax*
This crab spider moves about exclusively on sand and never occurs in vegetation. Its nest is a small bowl in sand lined with a white web and surrounded by a circular wall of sand particles spun together. The eggs, deposited here, are covered with threads to which additional sand grains are attached. In this way the egg mass is both camouflaged and protected against drying up. If the egg cocoon is placed near a straw, it is attached to this by threads. Spider, 327.

346 *Theridion saxatile*
The retreat of this spider is placed in the centre of its snare and consists mainly of sand grains which have been gathered singly from the ground. The spherical white egg cocoon is usually found in the retreat, but if the temperature there exceeds 40°C the egg cocoon is carried out and suspended near the outside of the web, where it can be some 10° cooler. Spider, 343.

347 *Araneus redii*
This round, moss-green ball, found attached to the tops of heather and grass, is the egg cocoon of the orb-spinner *Araneus redii*, a smaller

relative of the cross spider. Spider, 340.

GASTROPODA: Land Snails and Slugs

348 Slippery Moss-snail, *Cochlicopa lubricella*
Height, 4·5–5·5 mm. Shell pale yellow with a white lip. By far the largest of the five whorls is that nearest the lip. Found mainly in dry and sandy places among grass and leaves and at times seen in dunes, but can endure immersion for several hours. Generally distributed in Britain.

349 Chrysalis-snail, *Pupilla muscorum*
Height, 3–4 mm. Fairly thick-shelled with a thickened lip. Found on grass fields, littoral meadows and beaches with vegetation, where it occurs in vegetation at the edge of stones, under sticks and timber and in similar places. Feeds on dead and decomposing plant material. Viviparous.

350 *Columella aspera*
Height, up to 3 mm. Fairly thin-shelled. Found in deciduous and mixed forests, often in dry places, and one of the few snails found on heaths, although usually in small numbers. Occurs under branches and on the leaves of many different herbs, like bilberry, where it is thought to feed on lower vegetation (epiphytic algae, lichens, etc.).

351 *Vallonia excentrica*
2–2·5 mm wide. Found in grass and under timber near the beach, where it is fairly common.

352 *Nesovitrea hammonis*
Up to 4 mm wide. Common in many different acid and semi-dry microhabitats, such as dead leaves under birch, in bilberry and in dry grass. Has four thin transverse lines on the whorls.

353 Pellucid Glass-snail,
Vitrina pellucida
A form intermediate between snails and slugs. Part of the mantle projects from the shell and covers the back of the animal. The very thin and brittle shell is up to 5 mm wide. Living specimens are usually seen only in the six winter months. Found crawling among dead plant material in several different eco-systems, including sandy beaches with vegetation, littoral meadows, dunes and willow scrub. The young hatch in winter from eggs 1 mm across and live underground during summer. Glass snails have been found on the bodies of migrating birds.

354 Dusky Slug, *Arion subfuscus*
Length, to 6 mm. Occurs in hedgerows, mixed forests, birch woods, acid bogs and occasionally in moors. The breathing hole is situated just in front of the middle of the shell. Feeds on various plant material and fungi. The eggs, oval and about 3 mm in length, are deposited in clumps in sheltered places.

355 *Deroceras agreste* and *D. reticulatum*
Agreste is cream-coloured, slim and pointed at the back. A fairly lively slug occurring in somewhat dry places, especially grassland. *Reticulatum* usually has spots, is high in the body, somewhat compressed, relatively slow and leaves a trail of white slime. Found in littoral meadows and similar places.

356 Tawny Glass-snail,
Euconulus fulvus
Width 2·5–3 mm. Has a pyramidal shell, with raised spire. In Britain, found in numerous situations, including scrub near beaches and dunes. A closely related species is found in acid bogs.

357 Wrinkled Snail, *Helicella caperata*
Width, 7·5–10 mm. Widely distributed in Britain, but particularly abundant in the south coastal counties. Often in evidence in profusion after rain. Has a thick calcareous shell. Found in rather dry places with umbellifers and similar plants, in limestone quarries, gravel pits and in pasture near beaches.

BOTANICAL PLATES

At times flowering plants are found in dunes and on heaths and moors whose appearance differs from that of the same plants elsewhere. There might be malformation of inflorescences or of the apices of shoots, or swelling or shortening of stems. These distortions are usually galls and most of them are induced by parasitic insects or mites. Among the insects, the larvae of certain sawflies, gall-wasps and gall-midges typically cause these appearances, but the larvae of some flies, beetles and moths also promote them. In the following plates we show a number of gall formations found on the commoner dune, heath and moorland plants. We do not give examples of mines, as in previous books in the series. This does not suggest the total absence of mines in the plants, but normally these are particularly small, since duneland and moorland species tend to have small leaves.

JUNIPER

358 Shoot-gall
This gall is common in many situations where there are juniper bushes. The two outside whorls of leaves are clustered into a cylindrical gall 10–12 mm long. The innermost leaves form a pointed capsule in which the larval cell is found. The orange larva of the gall-midge *Oligotrophus juniperinus* feeds inside.

SEA COUCH

359 Cigar-gall
Can be recognized by the leaves which are compressed, as a result of shortening of the stem internodes, to form a cigar-shaped gall. Caused by the larva of the chalcid-wasp *Isthmosoma hyalipenne*, about 3–4 mm long. Larvae of frit-flies (e.g. 309) also cause cigar galls on sea couch and other grasses.

CREEPING WILLOW

360 Stem-gall
Causer, the sawfly *Euura atra*. The gall is oblong, spindle-shaped, 10–15 mm long and 5–7 mm wide and is usually sited asymmetrically on the twig. Generally only one larva colonizes each gall. At first white, this becomes pale green later and has a broad, clearly marked head. It eats a round hole in the gall to escape.

361 Leaf-gall
A spherical, bright red gall, about 10 mm across, caused by the sawfly *Pontania viminalis*. Always found on the undersides of leaves.

362 Leaf-gall
This spherical gall, thickly covered with fine hair, is caused by *Pontania pedunculi*, a close relative of the sawfly in the previous gall.

Also found on the underside of leaves, where it is never red.

363 Rosette-gall
Internodes of the shoot apex become markedly shortened, resulting in the formation of a rosette on various species of willow. The causer is the larva of the gall-midge *Rhabdophaga rosaria*, which feeds inside the stem tissues. Only one larva occurs in each gall.

364 Shoot-gall
The shoot apex takes the form of a leaf-rosette, approximately 10 mm long and 4 mm across, covered with silvery hair. Caused by the larva of the gall-midge *Rhabdophaga jaapi*. The imago emerges in spring.

365 Leaf-galls
Small pustulate galls, 1–2 mm long, usually on the upper sides of the leaves. On the underside is a hair-lined pore. Induced by the gall-mite *Eriophyes tetanothrix*.

BURNET ROSE

366 Leaf-gall
A gall which protrudes on both sides of the leaf and is either round or oblong in shape. Often several galls are found more or less attached to each other, their colour greenish or reddish and their surface smooth or covered with small thorns. Caused by the gall-wasp *Diplolepis* (=*Rhodites*) *spinosissimae*.

BROOM

367 Axillary-bud Galls
Green swellings, up to 12 mm long, in the leaf axils, induced in spring by the gall-midge *Asphondylia sarothamni*. The flowers do not open properly and later become black and die. The pod also is attacked.

368 Flower-bud Gall
The bud swells and the style protrudes from this. Caused by the pink larva of the gall-midge *Jaapiella sarothamni*.

NEEDLE FURZE

369 Shoot-gall
The shoot apex, round or oval with more or less swollen leaves, is covered with thick, white hair. The growth, found on several species of *Genista*, is caused by the gall-midge *Jaapiella genisticola*.

CROWBERRY

370 Shoot-gall
The shoot apex is shortened so that the leaves, which are malformed, smooth and discoloured, become clustered into a head. Caused by the gall-mite *Aceria* (=*Eriophyes*) *empetri*.

BEARBERRY

371 Bud-galls
The buds are enlarged and malformed by the gall-mite *Aceria* (=*Eriophyes*) *jaapi*.

THYME

372 Galled flowers
Inflorescences of thyme often resemble the illustration, with the
individual flowers converted into
cylinders covered by thick, whitish
hair. Caused by the gall-mite
Aceria (=*Eriophyes*) *thomasi*.

LADY'S BEDSTRAW

373 Shoot-gall
The shoot apex becomes a half-
open gall, about 8 mm across, the
shape of which is similar to that of
an artichoke. The leaves are up-
right, shortened and more or less
fleshy. The colour is initially reddish or violet and later brown.
Caused by the gall-midge *Dasyneura galiicola*. Several orange
larvae colonize a single gall.

374 Stem-gall
A very common gall induced by
the gall-midge *Geocrypta galii*. The
stem bears spherical or oblong
one-celled swellings, which are
spongy and more or less reddish.

375 Shoot-gall
The tops of the main or side shoots
end in an egg-shaped or spindle-
shaped gall, up to 15 mm long.

Often brownish-yellow in colour,
naked and hollow inside, the leaves
are not part of its formation as was
the case in 373. Caused by the gall-
mite *Aceria* (=*Eriophyes*) *galiobia*.

WORMWOOD

376 Stem-gall
The conspicuous oblong swellings
illustrated here are found on
various wormwood species and are
caused by moth larvae (microlepidoptera), usually by those of
the genus *Eucosma*.

377 Capitulum-gall
Shoots and inflorescences become
swollen, forming large egg-shaped
heads, several centimetres in diameter. In the centre of the head is
a cell with several compartments,
each containing one larva of the
gall-midge *Boucheella artemisiae*.

HAWKWEED

378 Stem-gall
Often found in the spikes of the
inflorescence, this gall is up to
30 mm long, spherical or barrel-
shaped, at first green in colour and
later brownish. A yellow-white
larva of the gall-wasp *Aulacidea
hieracii* is found in each cell.

BIBLIOGRAPHY

Useful references for further reading include the following books:

Beirne, B. P. *British Pyralid and Plume Moths*. Warne, 1954.

Cloudsley-Thompson, J. L. and Sankey, J. *Land Invertebrates*. Methuen, 1961.

Collyer, C. N. and Hammond, C. O. *Flies of the British Isles*. Warne, 1951.

Dale, A. *Patterns of Life*. Heinemann, 1960.

Darlington, A. *Natural History Atlas*. Warne, 1969. Outlines physical and chemical characteristics of some of the sandy ecosystems and suggests links between these and their colonizers, including vertebrates.

Fabre, J. H. *La Vie des Insectes*. Libraire Delagrave, Paris, 1920. A classic as valid today as when it was written, containing detailed and readable accounts from first-hand observation of the life-histories of several of the larger insects in the present book.

Imms, A. D. *Insect Natural History*. Collins (New Naturalist Series), 1947.

Kevan, D. K. McE. *Soil Animals*. Witherby, 1962.

Linssen, E. F. *Beetles of the British Isles*. Warne, 1959.

Locket, G. H. and Millidge, A. F. *British Spiders*. Ray Society, 1953.

Salisbury, E. J. *Downs and Dunes*. Bell, 1952. Required reading for anyone wishing to consider in detail the vegetation growing in the kinds of light soils included here.

Sandars, E. *An Insect Book for the Pocket*. Oxford University Press, 1946.

Savory, T. H. *The World of Small Animals*. University of London Press, 1955.

South, R. *The Butterflies of the British Isles*. Warne, 1928.

South, R. *The Moths of the British Isles*. Warne, 1943.

Southwood, T. R. E. and Leston, D. *Land and Water Bugs of the British Isles*. Warne, 1959.

Step, E. *Bees, Wasps, Ants and Allied Insects of the British Isles*. Warne, 1932.

INDEX

The items listed are in alphabetical order, both the Latin and the common names being included. The numbers refer to the illustration numbers.